Troubleshooting Citrix XenDesktop®

The ultimate troubleshooting guide for clear, concise, and real-world solutions to a wide range of common Citrix XenDesktop® problems

Gurpinder Singh

enterprise
professional expertise distilled

PUBLISHING

BIRMINGHAM - MUMBAI

Troubleshooting Citrix XenDesktop®

First published: October 2015

Production reference: 1201015

Published by Packt Publishing Ltd.
Livery Place
35 Livery Street
Birmingham B3 2PB, UK.

ISBN 978-1-78528-013-9

www.packtpub.com

Notice

Credits

Author
Gurpinder Singh

Reviewers
Mayur Arvind Makwana
Puthiyavan Udayakumar

Commissioning Editor
Dipika Gaonkar

Acquisition Editor
Larissa Pinto

Content Development Editor
Neeshma Ramakrishnan

Technical Editor
Taabish Khan

Copy Editor
Sneha Singh

Project Coordinator
Shweta H Birwatkar

Proofreader
Safis Editing

Indexer
Hemangini Bari

Production Coordinator
Nitesh Thakur

Cover Work
Nitesh Thakur

About the Author

Gurpinder Singh is an IT consultant with more than eight years of experience in the field of information technology. He has played various roles ranging from desktop support and system administration to virtualization expert with multiple Indian MNCs while working for clients all over the world.

He holds various enterprise renowned certifications from Microsoft and Citrix for managing, implementing, and troubleshooting Windows Server and Citrix virtualization products. During his eight years of work, he has worked for multiple global clients where he got the chance to work on projects that involved implementing high-end and complex virtualization projects.

He currently works for a large Indian IT MNC as a Citrix consultant and is involved in medium-to-large Citrix virtualization projects.

About the Reviewers

Mayur Arvind Makwana is a software IT specialist who holds a degree in computer engineering from India and has more than six years of experience in the field of information technology, covering Microsoft, Citrix, and VMware technologies. He is currently working on infrastructure operations for a Citrix (XenApp®/XenDesktop®) and Windows (WSUS/SCCM) project at one of the leading Fortune 500 companies. He is a huge believer in certification. His current certifications include the following:

- Citrix Certified Administrator for Citrix XenApp 6.5® (CCA)
- Microsoft Certified Professional (MCP)
- Microsoft Specialist (Microsoft Server Virtualization with Windows Server Hyper-V and System Center)
- VMware Certified Associate – Data Center Virtualization (VCA-DCV)
- ITIL (Information Technology Infrastructure Library) V3 foundation
- ChangeBase AOK (Application Compatibility Testing and Remediation)
- Oracle Certified Associate (OCA)

Mayur writes technical blogs on `www.all-about-software-applications-repackaging.com`. He has attended several courses and conducted training on topics such as the following:

- Licensing Windows Server
- Advanced Tools and Scripting with PowerShell 3.0 Jump Start
- Deploying Windows 8
- Licensing Windows 8
- Migrating from Windows XP to Windows 7
- Networking Fundamentals
- Introduction to Hyper-V Jump Start

He has also reviewed the following technical books for Packt Publishing:

- *Microsoft Application Virtualization Cookbook*, *James Preston*
- *Windows PowerShell for .NET Developers*, *Chendrayan Venkatesan and Sherif Talaat*
- *Getting Started with PowerShell*, *Michael Shepard*
- *Troubleshooting Citrix XenApp®*, *Stephen Paul* (work in progress)

I would like to thank my mom, Beena Makwana, who has always encouraged me to utilize my potential and help people by sharing my expertise and knowledge. Thanks to the Packt Publishing team for giving me this opportunity.

Puthiyavan Udayakumar has more than eight years of IT experience and has expertise in areas such as Citrix, VMware, Microsoft products, and Apache CloudStack. He has extensive experience in the field of designing and implementing virtualization solutions using various Citrix, VMware, and Microsoft products. He is an IBM Certified Solution Architect and a Citrix Certified Enterprise Engineer and has more than 16 certifications in infrastructure products. He has authored *Getting Started with Citrix CloudPortal™*, *Getting Started with Citrix Provisioning Services™ 7.0*, *VMware vSphere Network Virtualization Recipe Book*, and *VMware vSphere Design Essentials*. He holds a master's degree in science with a specialization in system software from the Birla Institute of Technology and Science (BITS), Pilani. He also has a bachelor's degree in engineering from SKR Engineering College, affiliated to the Anna University. He has also received a national award from the Indian Society for Technical Education (ISTE). He has presented various research papers that follow the IEEE pattern at more than 15 national and international conferences, including IADIS (held in Dublin, Ireland).

I would like thank Packt for giving me the opportunity to review this book.

Good luck to Packt and the author of this book.

www.PacktPub.com

Support files, eBooks, discount offers, and more

For support files and downloads related to your book, please visit www.PacktPub.com.

Did you know that Packt offers eBook versions of every book published, with PDF and ePub files available? You can upgrade to the eBook version at www.PacktPub.com and as a print book customer, you are entitled to a discount on the eBook copy. Get in touch with us at service@packtpub.com for more details.

At www.PacktPub.com, you can also read a collection of free technical articles, sign up for a range of free newsletters and receive exclusive discounts and offers on Packt books and eBooks.

https://www2.packtpub.com/books/subscription/packtlib

Do you need instant solutions to your IT questions? PacktLib is Packt's online digital book library. Here, you can search, access, and read Packt's entire library of books.

Why subscribe?

- Fully searchable across every book published by Packt
- Copy and paste, print, and bookmark content
- On demand and accessible via a web browser

Free access for Packt account holders

If you have an account with Packt at www.PacktPub.com, you can use this to access PacktLib today and view 9 entirely free books. Simply use your login credentials for immediate access.

Instant updates on new Packt books

Get notified! Find out when new books are published by following @PacktEnterprise on Twitter or the *Packt Enterprise* Facebook page.

Table of Contents

Preface

Citrix XenDesktop® is the leading solution of desktop virtualization that provides users with access to their favorite apps and desktops on any device, anywhere using Citrix Receiver™.

XenDesktop® brings the applications and desktops to the user in a bundle, presented and arranged in the form of catalogs. The user either needs a basic office application or a high-end engineering application that runs on a hosted desktop environment and it requires a proper planning of the network, server, and storage pieces to make it a successful VDI deployment.

Due to involvement of multiple layers in the XenDesktop® infrastructure design, it becomes essential for Citrix administrators to have a good understanding of these infrastructure pieces in order to manage and maintain the XenDesktop® environment.

This practical guide will give you clear, concise, and real-world troubleshooting instructions on a number of commonly faced Citrix XenDesktop® problems.

This book will provide you with the fundamental knowledge on desktop virtualization and XenDesktop® architecture. Each chapter in this book is focused on a specific troubleshooting area giving the users some time to learn and apply relevant tools and practices to troubleshoot the problems with a well-defined approach.

What this book covers

Chapter 1, Getting Started – Understanding Citrix XenDesktop® and its Architecture, provides a basic understanding of desktop virtualization concepts, architecture, new features in XenDesktop® 7.x, and XenDesktop® delivery models based on the FlexCast® technology involving Machine Creation Services and Provisioning Services™.

Chapter 2, Troubleshooting Toolkit for Citrix XenDesktop®, discusses all the tools that can help us in troubleshooting a Citrix XenDesktop® environment. We will also learn the importance of implementing these tools for different troubleshooting methodologies within the scope of XenDesktop® environments.

Chapter 3, Getting Around Installation Issues, discusses the troubleshooting of different installation issues arising in a XenDesktop® environment.

Chapter 4, Overcoming VDA Registration Problems, focuses on acquiring skills related to the VDA registration process and troubleshooting different kinds of VDA registration problems that you may encounter in a XenDesktop® environment.

Chapter 5, Conquering Citrix Session Launch Difficulties, focuses on learning the VDA launch process and its related problem areas that can help a Citrix administrator in troubleshooting different kinds of VDA launch problems that they may encounter in a XenDesktop® environment.

Chapter 6, Surpassing XenDesktop® Service Issues, explains the XenDesktop® services architecture and develops essential skills required to troubleshoot any service-related issues that arise in your XenDesktop® environment.

Chapter 7, Troubleshooting Performance, focuses on the basics of performance parameters, details on sizing for environment, and troubleshooting performance issues using Citrix and third-party tools.

Chapter 8, Solving Printing Issues, shows the basics of setting up the Citrix printing architecture, configuring printing policies, and troubleshooting printing issues.

Chapter 9, Getting the Better of HDX™ MediaStream Challenges, focuses on Citrix XenDesktop® HDX™ policies and their configuration, which is the key area to optimize performance in any XenDesktop® deployment.

Chapter 10, Taming MCS and PVS™ Setbacks Gracefully, focuses on troubleshooting common Machine Creation Services and Provisioning Services™ configuration issues that may arise in your Citrix XenDesktop® environment's daily operations.

Chapter 11, Troubleshooting NetScaler® Integration Issues, focuses on troubleshooting some common issues that you may encounter while integrating Citrix NetScaler® with your XenDesktop® environment to enable remote access for users.

Chapter 12, Dealing with Known Issues in Citrix XenDesktop®, highlights some general issues that have been identified and recorded by Citrix in their database that every admin must be aware of before starting with the troubleshooting of other Citrix XenDesktop® issues.

What you need for this book

The various software required to perform troubleshooting are as follows:

- Windows SDK for Windows 7 (Windows 2008 R2) or Windows 8 (Windows Server 2012)
- Citrix Studio™ and Director (these tools are part of the XenDesktop® installation suite)
- Microsoft ProcMon, Citrix CDFControl, HDX™ Monitor, Print Detective, StressPrinters, XDPing, XDDBDiag, Xperf, and Wireshark
- Microsoft Active Directory tools

Who this book is for

Troubleshooting Citrix XenDesktop® is intended to be an ultimate resource guide for all Citrix administrators or Citrix engineers who are working on Citrix XenDesktop® and have an intermediate to advance level of experience in designing, implementing, and troubleshooting the Citrix XenDesktop® product suite. Apart from Citrix XenDesktop®, the intended audience should have a good understanding and experience of Windows servers, Active Directory GPOs, DNS, DHCP, user profiles, Citrix XenApp®, Citrix Provisioning Services™, and related technical skills.

Conventions

In this book, you will find a number of text styles that distinguish between different kinds of information. Here are some examples of these styles and an explanation of their meaning.

Code words in text, database table names, folder names, filenames, file extensions, pathnames, dummy URLs, user input, and Twitter handles are shown as follows: "Type `help Get-<Alias>Service Status -Full` for more details."

A block of code is set as follows:

```
<system.diagnostics>
    <sources>
        <source name="System.ServiceModel"
```

Any command-line input or output is written as follows:

```
Test-Path $profile
```

New terms and **important words** are shown in bold. Words that you see on the screen, for example, in menus or dialog boxes, appear in the text like this: "Go to the **Attributes** tab and select SPN to edit the entry."

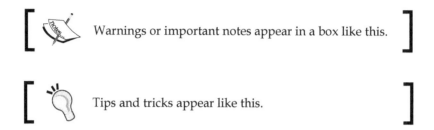

Warnings or important notes appear in a box like this.

Tips and tricks appear like this.

Reader feedback

Feedback from our readers is always welcome. Let us know what you think about this book—what you liked or disliked. Reader feedback is important for us as it helps us develop titles that you will really get the most out of.

To send us general feedback, simply e-mail feedback@packtpub.com, and mention the book's title in the subject of your message.

If there is a topic that you have expertise in and you are interested in either writing or contributing to a book, see our author guide at www.packtpub.com/authors.

Customer support

Now that you are the proud owner of a Packt book, we have a number of things to help you to get the most from your purchase.

Downloading the example code

You can download the example code files from your account at http://www.packtpub.com for all the Packt Publishing books you have purchased. If you purchased this book elsewhere, you can visit http://www.packtpub.com/support and register to have the files e-mailed directly to you.

Errata

Although we have taken every care to ensure the accuracy of our content, mistakes do happen. If you find a mistake in one of our books—maybe a mistake in the text or the code—we would be grateful if you could report this to us. By doing so, you can save other readers from frustration and help us improve subsequent versions of this book. If you find any errata, please report them by visiting `http://www.packtpub.com/submit-errata`, selecting your book, clicking on the **Errata Submission Form** link, and entering the details of your errata. Once your errata are verified, your submission will be accepted and the errata will be uploaded to our website or added to any list of existing errata under the Errata section of that title.

To view the previously submitted errata, go to `https://www.packtpub.com/books/content/support` and enter the name of the book in the search field. The required information will appear under the **Errata** section.

Piracy

Piracy of copyrighted material on the Internet is an ongoing problem across all media. At Packt, we take the protection of our copyright and licenses very seriously. If you come across any illegal copies of our works in any form on the Internet, please provide us with the location address or website name immediately so that we can pursue a remedy.

Please contact us at `copyright@packtpub.com` with a link to the suspected pirated material.

We appreciate your help in protecting our authors and our ability to bring you valuable content.

Questions

If you have a problem with any aspect of this book, you can contact us at `questions@packtpub.com`, and we will do our best to address the problem.

1
Getting Started – Understanding Citrix XenDesktop® and its Architecture

Before we get involved in learning the tools and concepts required for troubleshooting the Citrix XenDesktop environment, it's always a good idea to start from the basics. So, let's take a look at the basic concepts of XenDesktop and its architecture. Citrix XenDesktop is an Enterprise-grade application and desktop virtualization solution that gives Citrix administrators the ability to centrally manage and host applications and virtual machines in a datacenter while delivering to endusers a complete desktop high-definition (HDX) experience.

 HDX technology provides users with a high-definition experience for virtual apps and desktops, on any device or network with enhancements to work with voice, video, and 3D-graphics applications.

In a traditional desktop environment, system administrators often tend to restrict certain users from having administrative privileges to install and uninstall personal sets of software on the office desktops. To centrally manage the environment and enterprise applications, many system administrators often choose a terminal server environment to provide a stable and lockdown desktop environment using Citrix XenApp.

Desktop virtualization provides many advantages that are similar to the terminal server environment with additional features and the flexibility to lock down images using the shared image concept and persistent desktops for users who like to have administrative rights on their desktops.

In this chapter, we will cover:

- Desktop virtualization
- Hosted Shared Desktop versus Hosted Virtual Desktop
- The Citrix FlexCast delivery technology
- The modular framework architecture
- Machine creation services versus provisioning services
- What's new in XenDesktop 7.x?

Desktop virtualization

Wikipedia describes desktop virtualization as follows:

> *Desktop virtualization is a technology that separates the desktop environment hosted on a physical server in a Data Center from the client machine that is used by an end user to access it.*

In traditional desktop environments, computers run an operating system where applications are executed and the user interface is displayed on the computer screen. By introducing desktop virtualization, you can set up the desktop environment in such a way that it doesn't have any direct link between the physical layer, operating system, application software, and display.

Desktop virtualization based on Citrix XenDesktop works on a client-server model where users access virtual desktops hosted on a centrally managed physical host in a datacenter, as shown in the following diagram:

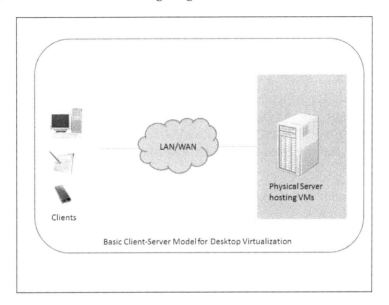

Desktop virtualization based on XenDesktop provides multiple benefits that are listed as follows:

- Anywhere, any-device access is available, for example, running the work environment on your home PC, Internet kiosk, tablet, mobile devices among others
- Multiple applications and operating systems can be supported without any conflicts among them
- Centralized management and provisioning
- Deliver data securely for your clients with data and network encryption

There are several vendors available to choose a desktop virtualization solution from, depending upon the organizational evaluation, needs, and requirements. Citrix is the market leader in application and desktop virtualization and has been in this area for almost the last two decades and is ruling it with its well-known product XenDesktop for desktop virtualization, which was officially released in the year 2007 as XenDesktop 2.0.

Hosted Shared Desktops (HSD) versus Hosted Virtual Desktops (HVD)

Instead of going through the XenDesktop architecture, we would like to explain the difference between the two desktop delivery platforms HSD and HVD. This is a common question that is asked by every system administrator whenever there is a discussion on the most suitable desktop delivery platform for the enterprises.

The selection of the desktop delivery platform depends on the requirements of the enterprise. Some choose Hosted Shared Desktops or server-based computing (XenApp) over Hosted Virtual Desktop (XenDesktop), where a single server desktop is shared between multiple users and the environment is locked using Active Directory GPOs.

XenApp is a cost-effective platform as compared to XenDesktop and many small to mid-sized enterprises prefer to choose XenApp due to its cost benefits and less complexity.

However, the preceding model does pose some risks to the environment as the same server is being shared by multiple users and a proper design plan is required to configure a proper HSD or XenApp published desktop environment.

Many enterprises have security and other user-level dependencies where they prefer to go with Hosted Virtual Desktop solutions. Hosted Virtual Desktop or XenDesktop runs on the Windows 7 or Windows 8 operating system as a virtual machine hosted on a datacenter. In this model, a single user connects to a single desktop and, therefore, there is a very low risk of the desktop configuration getting impacted for all users.

> XenDesktop 7.x and the preceding versions also enable you to deliver server-based desktops (HSD) along with HVD in one product suite. XenDesktop also provides HVD pooled desktops that work on a shared OS image concept that is similar to the HSD desktops with a difference of running a desktop operating system instead of a server operating system.

Let's take a look at the following table that will provide you with a fair idea of the requirements and recommendations of both the delivery platforms for your enterprise:

Customer Requirement	Delivery Platform
The user base needs to work on one or two applications and often need not do any updates or installations on their own.	Hosted Shared Desktop
The user base works on their own core set of applications for which they need to change system-level settings, installations, and so on.	Hosted Virtual Desktops (dedicated)
The user base works on MS Office and other content creation tools.	Hosted Shared Desktop
The user base needs to work on CPU and graphic-intensive applications that requires video rendering.	Hosted Virtual Desktop (Blade PCs)
The user base needs to have admin privileges to work on specific sets of applications.	Hosted Virtual Desktop (pooled)

You can always have a mixed set of desktop delivery platforms in your environment focused on the customer requirements.

The Citrix FlexCast® delivery technology

Citrix FlexCast is a delivery technology that allows the Citrix administrator to personalize virtual desktops to meet the performance, security, and flexibility requirements of endusers.

There are different types of user requirements; some need standard desktops with a standard set of apps while others require high-performance personalized desktops. Citrix has come up with a solution to meet these demands with the Citrix FlexCast technology.

You can deliver any kind of virtual desktop with the FlexCast technology; there are five different categories in which FlexCast models are available:

- Hosted Shared Desktop or HSD
- Hosted Virtual Desktop or HVD
- Streamed VHD
- Local VMs
- On-demand apps

A detailed discussion on these models is beyond the scope of this book. However, I have explained the difference between the Hosted Shared versus Hosted Virtual Desktop models in the last section. To read more about the FlexCast models, visit `http://support.citrix.com/article/CTX139331`.

The modular framework architecture

To understand the XenDesktop architecture, it's better to break it down into discrete independent modules, rather than visualizing it as a single integrated big piece. Citrix provides this modularized approach to design and architect XenDesktop to meet the end customer's set of requirements and objectives. This modularized approach solves the customer requirements by providing a platform that is highly resilient, flexible, and scalable.

This reference architecture is based on the information gathered by multiple Citrix consultants working on a wide range of XenDesktop implementations. You should take a look at the basic components of the XenDesktop architecture that everyone should be aware of before getting involved with troubleshooting:

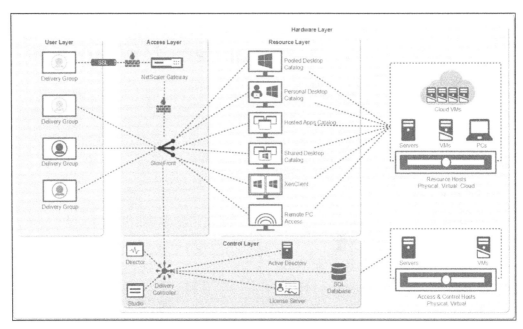

© Citrix Systems, Inc.

We will not spend much time on understanding each component of the reference architecture; you can refer to `http://www.citrix.com/content/dam/citrix/en_us/documents/products-solutions/xendesktop-deployment-blueprint.pdf` for more information, as this is out of the scope of this book. We will just go through each component quickly.

XenDesktop® and its architectural components

XenDesktop provides us with a desktop delivery platform by integrating several distributed components to deliver the best user experience for the VDI infrastructure.

The high level XenDesktop architecture includes the following key components:

- **Receiver**: The Citrix Receiver is a replacement of the Citrix ICA client, which you will have been using from the MetaFrame times. This was transformed from Program Neighborhood Agent to the Citrix Online plugin to the now so called Citrix Receiver.

- **HDX technology**: This provides the user with a high-definition experience for virtual apps and desktops on any devices and networks with enhancements to work with voice, video, and 3D graphic applications.

- **NetScaler Gateway**: Citrix NetScaler Gateway provides a secure remote access to users accessing the Citrix published apps and desktops from anywhere and on any device by connecting to Citrix Receiver.

- **Database**: Microsoft SQL Server is the only supported database.

- **License server**: You must already have been aware of this component for a long time. To work with the Citrix range of products, you must have at least one Citrix License server in your environment, to provide you with the Citrix licenses.

- **Virtual Delivery Agent (VDA)**: The Virtual Desktop Agent needs to be installed on the virtual machines to which all the users will be connected. It enables the machines to register themselves with the controllers and manage the HDX connection between the machines and the user devices. There are two types of VDA agents available:
    - VDA agent for the Windows Server OS
    - VDA agent for the Windows Desktop OS

- **StoreFront**: Citrix StoreFront is the replacement of the Citrix Web Interface product. It provides a similar functionality with some enhancements that provide access to published apps or desktops as per user needs.

- **XenDesktop Controller**: Access to all the apps and desktops are centrally managed by the Controller server.

- **Citrix Director**: The Director provides a real-time dashboard supplying diagnostic information for users, applications, and desktops. This is commonly used as the first level of troubleshooting.

- **EdgeSight**: If you require historical trending data for analysis and performance, then EdgeSight is the tool for you provided by Citrix, free of cost, with the Platinum license. You can also look at the more capable tool provided by Citrix, until recently called Citrix Insight, which succeeded EdgeSight.

- **Citrix Studio**: It's one of the management consoles that provide a simple GUI interface to create and manage desktops and apps.

 For detailed information on the XenDesktop architecture, please read *Getting Started with XenDesktop 7.x, Craig Thomas Ellrod, Packt Publishing*.

MCS versus PVS™

Anyone who has worked on XenDesktop will have definitely heard the terms: MCS and PVS. You have to choose either MCS or PVS to deploy VDI in an Enterprise environment. This is one of the major concerns for every organization, which they would like to be answered by a Citrix solution architect while working on a desktop virtualization project:

Which delivery technology is better, MCS or PVS?

Now, let's start by learning some basics about these two technologies.

Machine Creation Service (**MCS**) provides the simplest functionality for the creation and maintenance of desktop catalogs. A step-by-step walkthrough on how to create/configure this feature can be found in the XenDesktop 7.x install guide. You can easily download this guide from http://www.citrix.com.

MCS-based deployment will have the following characteristics:

- A master image is prepared from a standard VM with all the customized apps and software that an admin wants in his virtual desktop.

- A master image file (.vmdk or .vhd depending on the supported hypervisors Hyper-V, XenServer, or VMware ESXi) is stored in the central datastores attached to the hypervisor pool.

- The admin provides custom settings for vCPU, memory, HDD, and many more.

- VMs are created as linked clones with at least two disks attached to them; a base OS disk and a personality disk containing the machine-related information.

- One difference disk will be attached to the VMs that are used to store and write the information to the VM. The disk used is as thin as provisioned (it needs to be checked for storage compatibility, if it is supported) and the disk size will grow along with your base disk to the maximum if required.

- A personal vDisk can also be attached to each VM to store persistent changes for users.

There are four types of resource catalog that MCS offers:

- **Pooled-Random**: This is most commonly used for standard users. Here, the desktops are assigned randomly. When the user logs off, the desktop becomes free and is available for another user. Any changes made to the desktops are undone on reboot.

- **Pooled-Static**: These desktops are for task workers who need the same desktop every time they log on. These desktops are assigned to a single user and on user logoff this desktop is not free for other users. On rebooting, any changes made to these desktops are undone like Pooled-Random.

- **Dedicated or personal desktops**: These desktops are meant to provide persistence to users and are recommended for task workers who need their own set of apps and control on their desktops. These are permanently assigned to a single user. When the user logs off, these desktops are not available in the pool for other users. All the changes made remain intact with subsequent reboots.

- **XenApp based Shared Desktops**: You have been using these desktops since the old MetaFrame Presentation server model. These are the hosted server-based published desktops where the server desktop is made available to the users to be shared with a set of users simultaneously.

You can also club pooled desktops with a personal vDisk to provide persistency to user-level changes.

The following diagram outlines the basic architecture of MCS:

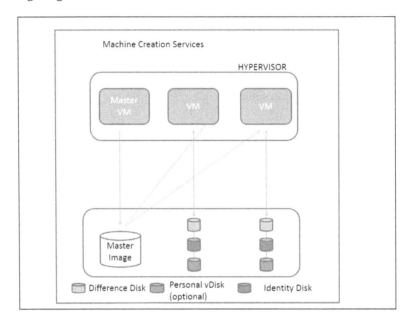

Provisioning Service (PVS) infrastructure is a result of Citrix acquiring Ardence, which is based out of Virginia, US. Ardence developed a boot program called the Ardence boot program that works on the PXE TFTP technology on which PVS streaming works. If you have worked on PVS previously, you must have heard of the major component ARDBP32.BIN being used for streaming in PVS, it still has the first three initials from Ardence.

PVS is a software streaming technology that Citrix uses to provide on-demand streaming of operating system content in real time from a single shared-disk residing anywhere on the network. Apart from the on-demand streaming, PVS simplifies image management as you don't have to manage images separately. Single-image management simplifies everything and you don't need to purchase any desktop deployment tools to manage this image.

Provisioning Services manages all writes to the vDisks with PVS write cache when using a vDisk in Standard mode (it is often called the read-only mode). You can configure the location of your write cache as follows:

- Cache on provisioning server (with or without persistence)
- Cache on target device RAM
- Cache on target device RAM with overflow to HDD
- Cache on target device hard drive (with or without persistence)

One of the most commonly used methods to store a write cache is to store it in the target device hard drive. There is a very good reason to follow this approach as it keeps the write location close to the target device, which actually minimizes the additional load on the PVS servers and also minimizes the load on the network.

Refer to the following diagram for the basic PVS architecture:

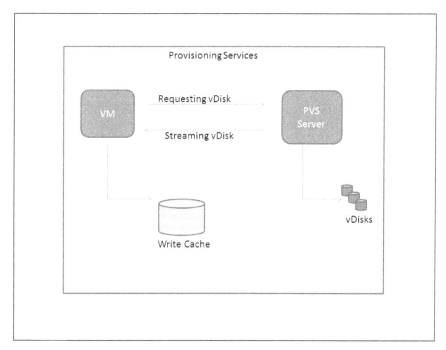

PVS architecture

Refer to the following diagram for the basic PVS communication flow:

	1	DHCP Discover	DHCP Server Options Option 66 – PVS IP Option 67 – ARDBP32.BIN
	2	DHCP Offer Option 66 and 67 offer	DHCP
	3	DHCP Request	
Target Device	4	DHCP ACK Option 66 and 67 sent	
	5	TFTP Read Request Port 69	Citrix PVS TFTP Service
	6	TFTP Data sent ARDBP32.BIN	Citrix PVS TFTP Service
	7	PVS Logon Process	Citrix Stream Service
	8	Streaming Process starts	

PVS communication flow

A PVS-based device can have three types of disks attached to it:

- The base OS shared disk is placed at the central PVS vDisk store and is streamed on each VM using PXE boot or BDM. You won't find this disk on the VM configuration on hypervisor, as this is streamed to VM either via PXE boot using either TFTP from a vDisk store or using BDM ISO.

 Boot device manager (**BDM**) is a utility that provides an optional method for providing IP and boot information to target devices. With this method, when the target device is booted, it fetches the boot information directly from the boot device. So, the target device would use this information to locate and boot from the required provisioning server.

- The write cache disk, unless you have set the write cache on the PVS server or the device RAM.
- A personal vDisk.

XenDesktop offers four types of resource catalog with PVS. The first three are the same as the first three resource catalogs that MCS offers, which we covered earlier in this section; that is, **Pooled-Random**, **Pooled-Static**, and **XenApp-based Shared Desktops**. The last one is **Remote PC Access**, which is a regular Windows desktop that is assigned to a single user which can be accessed locally or remotely.

We can utilize a personal vDisk or persistent cache to permanently store the changes made by users. The changes remain permanent after reboot as well.

What's new in XenDesktop® 7.x?

With the release of Citrix XenDesktop 7, Citrix has introduced a lot of improvements over the previous releases. With every new product release, there is a lot of information published and sometimes it becomes very difficult to get the key information that all the system administrators will be looking for in order to understand what has been changed and what are the key benefits of the new release.

The purpose of this section is to highlight the new key features that XenDesktop 7.x brings to the fore for all Citrix administrators.

 This section does not provide you with all the details regarding the new features and changes that XenDesktop 7.x has introduced but highlights the key points that every Citrix administrator should be aware of while administrating XenDesktop 7.

The key highlights of XenDesktop 7.x are as follows:

- XenApp and XenDesktop are now a part of a single setup
- Cloud integration to support desktop deployments on the cloud
- The IMA database doesn't exist anymore
- The IMA is replaced by **FlexCast Management Architecture (FMA)**
- Zone concept—there are no more zones or ZDC (data collectors)
- Database support—Microsoft SQL is the only supported database
- Sites are used instead of farms
- Console integration—XenApp and XenDesktop can now share consoles; Citrix Studio and Desktop Director are used for both products
- Shadowing feature is deprecated; Citrix recommends Microsoft Remote Assistance for use

- Locally installed applications integrated to be used with server-based desktops
- HDX and mobility features
- Profile management is included
- MCS can now be leveraged for both server and desktop OS
- MCS now works with KMS
- Storefront replaces Web Interface
- Remote PC access
- No more Citrix streaming Profile Manager; Citrix recommends that you use MS App-V
- XenApp installation—core component is replaced by a VDA agent

Summary

We now have a basic understanding of desktop virtualization concepts, architecture, new features in XenDesktop 7.x, and XenDesktop delivery models based on the FlexCast technology that involve Machine Creation Services and Provisioning Services.

Our next chapter will focus on introducing the troubleshooting toolkit that is a must for every Citrix administrator who wants to learn to troubleshoot XenDesktop.

2
Troubleshooting Toolkit for Citrix XenDesktop®

In the first chapter, we gained a basic knowledge of Citrix XenDesktop and its architecture and, with this knowledge, we can now identify the different components used in the XenDesktop architecture very easily. Now, we are ready to start learning about some basic tools and methodologies that we can use in troubleshooting Citrix XenDesktop issues.

This chapter will start with highlighting a common Citrix methodology and third-party tools that are used to troubleshoot Citrix XenDesktop issues; it will be followed up by the knowledge of all the required Citrix and third-party tool configuration and analysis required to build a strong foundation required for troubleshooting.

The knowledge gained in this chapter will help us in understanding and analyzing the case studies that will be shared randomly throughout the book.

In this chapter, we will cover:

- Working with Citrix Studio and Desktop Director
- Working with CDFControl
- Working with DDC/VDA agent logging and PortICA log
- Working with Perfmon and Procmon
- Understanding HDX Monitor
- Exploring Citrix Scout and Citrix Quick Launch
- Getting familiar with Print Detective and StressPrinters

- Working with the Site Checker Tool
- Exploring XDPing and XDDBDiag
- Working with Xperf and Wireshark
- Working with the PowerShell SDK for XenDesktop

Citrix Studio (Desktop Studio)

Citrix has been working hard for the last few years to simplify its consoles and we must say that they have succeeded in this with the release of XenDesktop 7.x. Thanks to their efforts in this area, we now have just two consoles to effectively carry out all our primary duties with Studio and Director.

Citrix Studio is one of the Citrix management consoles provided with the Citrix XenDesktop suite that all Citrix administrators will be using to configure and deliver apps and desktops for their enterprise environment.

You can organize your resources in the form of machine catalogs, delivery groups, and also provide access to delegated administrators.

Citrix Studio is installed by default on all the Citrix Desktop Delivery Controllers. The initial configuration for the creation of site and database connections is established using this console.

 You can also automate site and database creation using PowerShell scripts.

You can also configure secure RemotePC access to physical PCs for users using this console.

Please refer to the following screenshot of the Citrix Studio interface, which we will be discussing to help us understand the console's options and functions for administration:

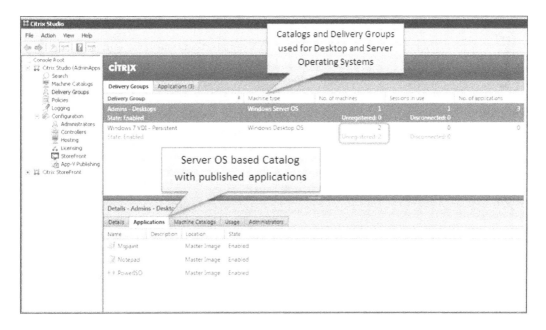

In the preceding screenshot, we can see some basic settings that every administrator will look at when seeing this console for the first time and also while trying to create and manage machine catalogs.

In the previous chapter, we discussed XenDesktop catalogs that MCS and PVS offer; so here we have created two basic catalogs, one for the server-based OS and the other for desktop-based OS.

While creating a machine catalog and adding machines to their dedicated delivery groups, you need to make sure that the new machine, whether it's server- or desktop-based, allocated to your delivery group is properly registered with the XenDesktop controller. You must have noticed in the preceding screenshot that, in the **Windows 7 VDI** desktop catalog, 2 machines are allocated and both of them are shown as unregistered in the console.

This is the starting point for an administrator working on XenDesktop sites. So, this is your first tool where you should be looking whether you can launch your desktops and applications or not. The unregistered state signifies that your machine is not able to contact the Delivery Controller and register itself.

> There is a chapter focused on VDA registration issues; we will explore these issues and how to resolve them later in *Chapter 4, Overcoming VDA Registration Problems*.

Some other key areas in the Studio console that you should be aware of are the **Licensing** and **StoreFront** tabs. These can help you in identifying licensing and StoreFront store-related issues in one place without any need to go to individual consoles:

> To know more about all the relevant settings of the Citrix Studio console and the initial configuration and setup, you should read the article at https://www.packtpub.com/virtualization-and-cloud/getting-started-xendesktop%C2%AE-7x.

The Director console (Desktop Director)

The Director is the primary tool for helpdesk administrators to troubleshoot basic issues within the XenDesktop environment. This console has been improved by Citrix in their last few releases and it has only gotten better.

With Director 7, you can now integrate Citrix NetScaler Insight to resolve session performance issues. You can view HDX NetScaler Insight in Director views and easily identify whether the issue is related to network.

 Please note that the HDX Insight integration feature is for Citrix Platinum customers only. To read more on HDX Insight, please download the NetScaler HDX Insight deployment guide from `https://www.citrix.com/content/dam/citrix/en_us/documents/products-solutions/netscaler-insight-center-deployment-and-sizing-guide.pdf`.

Director comes with a very informative dashboard displaying the relevant diagnostic details of your XenDesktop infrastructure. Please refer to the following screenshot of the Director dashboard:

The preceding screenshot of the dashboard shows the details of failed machines, user connection failures, established sessions, licensing issues, the current capacity, and logon duration among many others. The data is updated every minute on the console.

The Director console provides two detailed views that can help helpdesk technicians in identifying and troubleshooting issues. We will go through each of the views and understand their functionality and the data they provide to administrators.

The Filters view

Basic troubleshooting begins with digging into the user session details. The dashboard provides sufficient information on connected and failed sessions. If you click on **Sessions Connected** or **User Connection Failures**, it will automatically take you to the **Filters** view for the session details; an example is shown in the following screenshot:

Similarly, you can click on the failed connections and see the details of all the connection failures under the **Filters** view, as shown in the following screenshot:

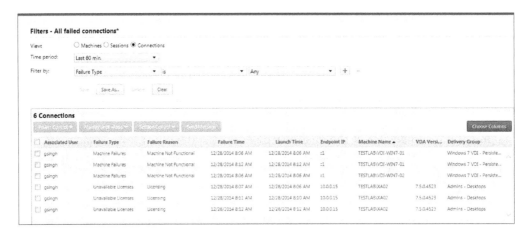

The **Filters** view provides you with all the required details for the failures, such as failure reason, time of failure, machines affected, and other relevant details. You can select columns to get more details on the failures. This is really useful for helpdesk staff; they can look at these events and take the necessary actions at their level to resolve these issues.

You can also get the details of the machines by selecting the **Machines** radio button under this view.

The Trends view

The dashboard provides the data of the last hour, so it is really good to have some historical data to look at and that can provide you with more details for the past week or past month. Administrators can click on **Trends** on the dashboard and will be redirected to the **Trends** view on the Director console. Please have a look at the following screenshot for reference:

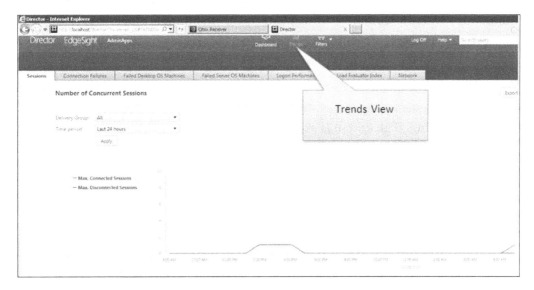

Here, you can select the time period to view the historical trends for the sessions, connection failures, failed desktop or server machines, logon performance, load evaluators, and network details.

By using these two views, the helpdesk staff can easily identify basic issues for desktop connections and troubleshoot/fix them.

CDFControl

Citrix Diagnostic Facility, or simply CDF, has been around since 2007 and is still considered to be the most used diagnostic tool by Citrix administrators. It has been recently added into Citrix Scout; however, you can still download it as an individual utility from `https://www.citrix.com`. This tool works well with all the latest releases of Citrix XenDesktop.

CDFControl is an event-tracing utility that is made to capture all Citrix-related diagnostic information and that gets its output from Citrix subsystem DLLs. You need to have local administrator rights on the system to start an event trace.

 To download and setup Citrix CDFControl for the first time, please visit `http://support.citrix.com/article/CTX111961`.

It's always recommended to have a trace captured before opening a case with Citrix because they will always ask for the capture as the first thing.

Once downloaded, you can run `CDFControl.exe` from the specified folder on the system to take your first trace. It will present you with the GUI interface showing multiple modules, to select from and start your trace.

It also provides a list of trace categories to simplify administrator needs for troubleshooting. If an admin is experiencing issues with FMA services, he can select the **Delivery Controller Services** module or, if there is an issue with application enumeration or launch, he can select the **Application Enum/Launch** module category.

Please refer to the following screenshot showing the GUI interface:

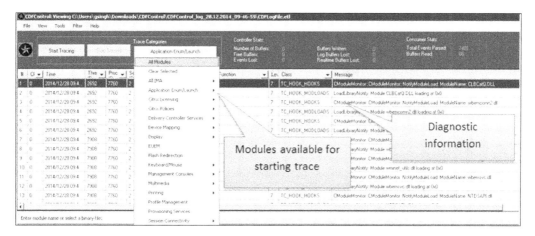

To capture a valid trace, you should start your trace, reproduce your issue, and then stop the trace. The trace will provide you with an ETL file in the same folder where you have configured the CDFControl utility.

You can open the trace file with the CDFControl utility by going to the **File** menu and selecting **Parse Trace**:

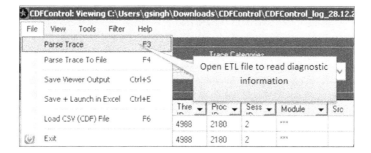

You will also need to download **trace message format** (**TMF**) files that are responsible for carrying out the instructions to parse and format the binary trace messages generated by CDFControl.

Using CDFControl, you can easily download TMF files, as shown in the following screenshot:

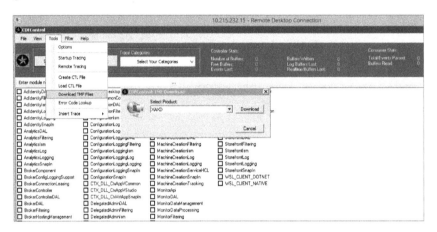

Once the files are downloaded, go to the **CDFControl Trace Settings** window and configure the path for downloaded TMF files and the path for the online TMF server:

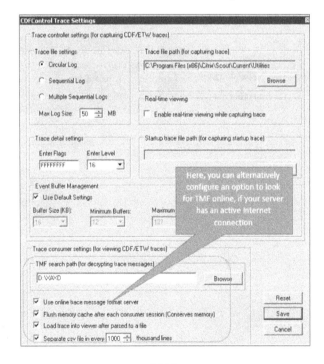

Now, you are all set up to parse and analyze the log files to find faults and issues within your XenDesktop environment:

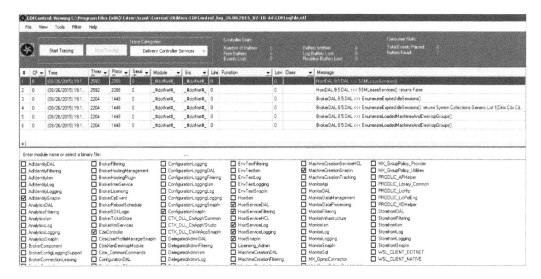

 When troubleshooting XenDesktop issues and selecting the **Delivery Controller Services** module, all the services are covered except one: the PortICA service (also called `PicaSvc2.exe`, the new name given to it by Citrix).

`PicaSvc2.exe` is one of the most important services when you are troubleshooting Citrix XenDesktop issues. This service is a part of your desktop OS on the virtual machine, Blade, or remote PCs. This service is responsible for all communications happening on your VDA machine except for communication with the Delivery Controller, handled by the Citrix Desktop service.

So, you must enable service logging while troubleshooting XenDesktop issues. This can be enabled by two methods. The first method is to create an XML file on the VDA machine and edit the configuration file to allow logging.

 You can find the procedure by referring to the Citrix article at `http://support.citrix.com/article/CTX118837`.

The second method is to do it via Citrix Scout; you can remotely enable PortICA logging while taking the CDF trace using Citrix Scout, as shown in the following screenshot:

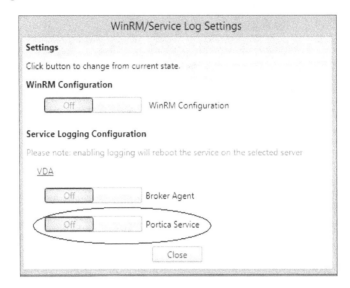

Configuring logging for XenDesktop®

To troubleshoot all the issues arising in the XenDesktop environment, you should be aware of what is cooking under the hood of the XenDesktop architecture. For this purpose, enabling service logging, VDA agent logging, and Controller logging is very essential and the key point here.

Service-based logging can be enabled via the command line or by using Citrix Scout, which is installed by default on XenDesktop 7.5 and later versions. Citrix Scout lacks some feature logging capability; it doesn't enable Citrix Broker Service agent logging.

So, it's always better to enable your environment's service-based logging using the command line or PowerShell:

An example command to enable Citrix Broker Service log is as follows:

```
BrokerService.exe –Logfile "C:\XDLogs\Citrix Broker
Service.log"
```

You need to run this command from the CMD prompt while in the appropriate service directory, which is `C:\Program Files\Citrix\ Broker\Service`.

After you have successfully configured the logging for all services, it's time to configure the VDA agent and PortICA logging, which are considered as most important for the XenDesktop infrastructure.

To enable VDA agent logging and PortICA logging, please read the Citrix article at http://support.citrix.com/article/ CTX117452.

You can also use the Citrix Log Enabler utility to enable controller level logging; please visit http://support.citrix.com/article/ CTX127492 for more information.

Please make sure that you disable XD logging once you are done with troubleshooting. Otherwise, it may eat up space on your servers.

Perfmon and Procmon

If you are a Windows or Citrix administrator, you might have heard the terms Perfmon and Procmon before. These are Microsoft tools that have been around from the NT era and have been used by all administrators for their daily troubleshooting issues.

Perfmon or **Performance Monitor** is used to monitor system performance such as CPU, memory, and network bandwidth being used by an operating system, applications, services, and so on. Perfmon is installed by default during Windows installation.

Procmon or **Process Monitor** is a free tool provided by Microsoft Sysinternals. The tool is used to monitor real-time activity of all the processes on the Windows platform. It combines two old tools called **RegMon** and **FileMon**, used to track registry and file access activities.

Procmon can be used to track failed attempts against accessing the registry, file shares, detect file errors, critical system processes, and many more.

Configuring Perfmon

Perfmon is installed by default on all Windows servers. To configure Perfmon, you can launch it by going to **All Programs** | **Administrative Tools** | **Performance Monitor** or simply by typing perfmon in the **Run** window.

Perfmon comes with a default system performance counter set to monitor CPU utilization, as shown in the following screenshot:

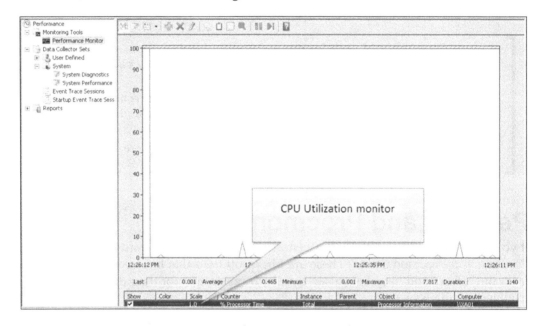

To configure Perfmon to capture all relevant performance parameters, we need to configure the data collector set to add all the relevant performance counters. Microsoft provides a built-in user level data collector set that comes with Windows 2008 Server as Server Manager Performance monitor.

If you just want to monitor CPU and memory performance, this data collector set will provide you with sufficient information:

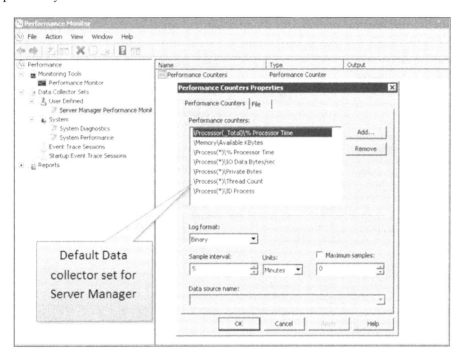

However, to configure advanced data collector sets to monitor performance counters that are not limited to CPU, memory, or network, you need to add relevant counters to your customized data collector set.

Please refer to the following screenshot of a customized data collector set to be used to monitor CPU, memory, paging file utilization, ICA connections, ICA session latency, Citrix Profile Management logon/logoff duration, HDX Flash input/output data bandwidth, and more:

The data collector set can capture all the parameters for server performance, logon/logoff duration, HDX MediaStream bandwidth and much more.

In today's world, this tool is rarely used by Citrix administrators to get performance-related data, as Citrix Director can provide you with the relevant data and you don't even need to spend time in configuring these data sets.

However, I still recommend this tool to advanced administrators who want to explore all the built-in counters provided by Microsoft and Citrix to play around. Sometime, the advanced tools such as Citrix Director or EdgeSight don't provide you with all the details you need for troubleshooting; configuring the right counters with this tool can point you in the right direction.

XenDesktop 7.x has a sizable number of built-in performance counters that can serve as a great tool for troubleshooting. Please refer to the following list of XenDesktop Perfmon counters that you can use on the XenDesktop environment for troubleshooting.

- Citrix Broker Service: Brokered Sessions
- Citrix Broker Service: Database Avg. Transaction Time
- Citrix Broker Service: Database Connected
- Citrix Broker Service: Database Transaction Errors/sec
- Citrix Broker Service: Database Transactions/sec
- Citrix Broker Service: Deregistration Requests
- Citrix Broker Service: Expired Launches/sec
- Citrix Broker Service: Expired Registrations/sec
- Citrix Broker Service: Ping Requests
- Citrix Broker Service: Hard Registrations/sec
- Citrix Broker Service: Registration Avg. Request Time
- Citrix Broker Service: Registration Rejects/sec
- Citrix Broker Service: Registration Requests/sec
- Citrix Broker Service: Soft Registrations/sec
- Citrix ADIdentity Service: Database Connected
- Citrix ADIdentity Service: Database Transaction Errors/sec
- Citrix Configuration Logging: Database Connected
- Citrix Configuration Logging: Database Transaction Errors/sec
- Citrix Configuration Service: Database Connected
- Citrix Configuration Service: Database Transaction Errors/sec
- Citrix Delegated Admin: Database Connected
- Citrix Delegated Admin: Database Transaction Errors/sec
- Citrix Environment Test: Database Connected
- Citrix Environment Test: Database Transaction Errors/sec
- Citrix Host Service: Database Connected
- Citrix Host Service: Database Transaction Errors/sec
- Citrix Machine Creation Service: Database Connected
- Citrix Machine Creation Service: Database Transaction Errors/sec
- Citrix Monitor: Database Connected
- Citrix Monitor: Database Transaction Errors/sec
- Citrix Storefront: Database Connected
- Citrix Storefront: Database Transaction Errors/sec

The counter details have been fetched directly from Perfmon available on the XenDesktop Controller server. To read more about XenApp/XenDesktop performance counters, please download the article at `http://support.citrix.com/servlet/KbServlet/download/30998-102-686964/Operations%20Guide%20-%20Monitoring.pdf`.

The document is outdated and won't provide you with much detail on recent releases of the XenDesktop/XenApp product line. However, the document is still considered as a good read for the information it contains on the performance monitors required to monitor Citrix infrastructure.

Configuring Procmon

Process Monitor is a free tool from Microsoft and can be easily downloaded from `http://download.sysinternals.com/files/ProcessMonitor.zip`.

This tool serves as a great asset in terms of troubleshooting application failures, file system issues, registry issues, boot logging, reading the application stack, and so on.

Once you have downloaded the tool, you will have three files named `Procmon.exe`, `procmon.chm`, and `Eula`.

- `Procmon.exe`: This is the utility setup file
- `procmon.chm`: This is the software helper file
- `Eula`: This is the Microsoft End User License Agreement

Procmon comes as a portable utility that doesn't require installation. You can run `Procmon.exe` directly by accepting the `Eula` screen and it will start capturing, as shown in the following screenshot for reference:

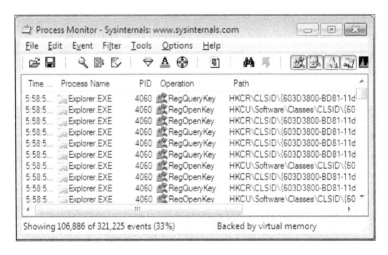

We have now downloaded Procmon and it is ready to take our first capture. Before we actually start looking at the capture log, we should have a basic understanding of the Procmon toolbar. Please have a look at the following Procmon toolbar screenshot to understand the basic toolbar features that can help us in analyzing the Procmon logs:

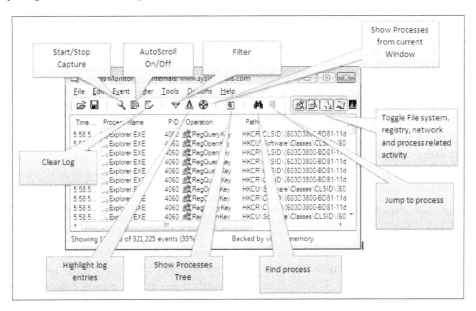

Procmon log data

To run this tool, you should be a part of the local administrator group on the local machine. Once the tool is launched, it immediately starts capturing three system-level activities: filesystem, registry, and process.

- **Filesystem**: Procmon captures the filesystem activity for all Windows filesystems whether it's a local storage or remote file share. The activity is monitored relative to the logged-on user session. You can deselect the filesystem activity by clicking on the filesystem activity button on the toolbar.

- **Registry**: Procmon captures all registry operations and the information is displayed using the Windows registry conventional path (**HKLM**: HKEY_ LOCAL_MACHINE). You can deselect the registry activity by clicking on the registry activity button on the toolbar.

- **Process**: Procmon captures all process-related information starting from the process and thread monitoring subsystem to creation and exit operations including DLL and device driver load operations. You can deselect the process activity by clicking on the process activity button on the toolbar.

We have gained a basic understanding of the Procmon tool, toolbar features, and relevant data that the Procmon log provides.

To understand the importance of this tool with respect to troubleshooting of Citrix environment, we are going to do a case study that is focused on troubleshooting slow logons of Citrix published desktops based on XenApp.

Case study – troubleshooting slow logons with Procmon

Problem description:

Users have been complaining about slow logons while logging to Citrix desktops. The desktops logins were taking approximately 3-5 minutes to show up on the desktop interface of the users.

Environment:

XenApp 6.5, Citrix Profile Manager 3.2.2, and ICA Online Plug-in 12.1.44.1

Troubleshooting analysis:

On initial diagnosis, we found that the slowness was experienced by the users intermittently. Some users were able to login within 30-50 seconds and some users were experiencing a delay of 3-4 minutes.

We started with checking the event viewer logs for the machines that were experiencing delays, but couldn't find any relevant error that could lead us to the cause of delay. We enabled UPM logging and GPO logging to understand the delay but there were no errors or warnings that were causing this delay.

To enable Citrix **User Profile Manager** (**UPM**), please visit the Citrix Knowledge Center article at http://support.citrix.com/ article/CTX126723.

To enable GPO logging, please refer to the MS article at http:// blogs.technet.com/b/csstwplatform/archive/2010/11/09/ how-to-enable-gpo-logging-on-windows-7-2008-r2.aspx.

As the next troubleshooting step, before involving Citrix, we went ahead and used the Procmon tool to capture the entire logon process for impacted users. However, we had to run this tool multiple times to capture a valid trace for impacted users.

While analyzing the logon process, we found that the freeze happens among 2-3 process threads, which indicated that the thread was waiting for network restoration. It led us to find out whether any network drives were mapped for users that were no longer accessible or if it was waiting for any network printers to be mapped.

I checked and found that the issue is with the network printer's mapping while the user is logging on to the Citrix desktop.

Resolution:

We changed the published desktop application setting from the Citrix AppCenter console so that it doesn't wait for the network printers to be mapped while logging in, which resolved the issue.

After modifying this application setting, the login time reduced from 3-5 minutes to just 15-20 seconds.

Similarly, Procmon can be used while troubleshooting slow logons, application failures, file access permission issues, and more.

HDX™ Monitor

Citrix has invested a lot of time and money in improving its products to provide a high-definition experience to its customers by introducing HDX technologies. With HDX, it had become essential to properly configure these features on your XenDesktop and XenApp environments. Many administrators faced real challenges in understanding whether the Citrix policies that are enabled for HDX features really work or not.

It had become difficult to isolate the issues related to HDX and sometimes, configuring HDX policies incorrectly caused the user experience to be impacted badly resulting in session choppiness and delayed mouse and keyboard response.

So, to help its customers, Citrix has released this wonderful tool called HDX Monitor for XenApp and XenDesktop. The latest version of this tool has come up with some new features that allow administrators to customize the metrics required to troubleshoot.

The tool can be downloaded from `https://taas.citrix.com/hdx/download/`.

The HDX Monitor tool is used to diagnose and monitor the activity of VDA and its features, analyze the data, and issue alerts on the console to make you aware about incorrect configuration and performance. The home screen looks like this:

Let's discuss the basic features and functionality that the HDX monitor provides to administrators:

- **Adobe Flash**: This is used to monitor and troubleshoot Flash redirection issues. A red cross on the screenshot suggests that Flash is either not installed or not working correctly. You can click on Adobe Flash and it will show you the detailed description of the issue. Please refer to the following screenshot for details:

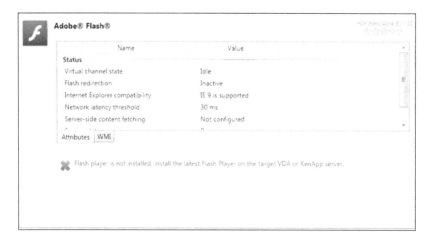

- **Audio**: This is used to know if audio redirection is enabled and is working fine.

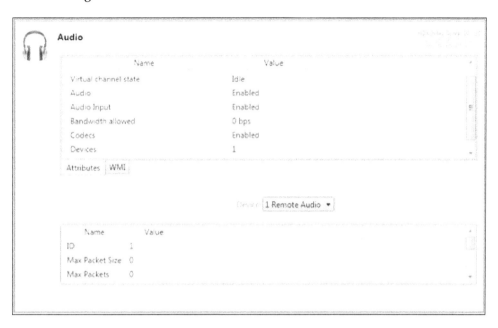

- **Client**: This component is used to monitor if the right client is installed and compatible with handling all HDX policies.

- **Graphics - Thinwire**: The graphics component provides information about the configuration set in the XenApp and XenDesktop environment for graphics and it also captures the network performance of Graphics Thinwire.

  This is one of the most important components in the HDX Monitor tool, as many Citrix administrators face challenges while configuring the right set of policies to be used to deliver HDX experience to endusers.

  The following information is key and worth noting:

  - Max FPS
  - Min FPS
  - Frames per second
  - Progressive display
  - Adaptive display
  - Extra color compression
  - Heavyweight JPEG

Let's have a look at the new graphics settings that come with XenDesktop 7.x:

Policy	Default Setting	Achievement
Legacy graphics mode	Off	To revert to first generation Adaptive Display.
Frame rate (FPS)	30	Sets max FPS (60 FPS supported on latest version).
Image quality	Medium	To adjust the level of compression for newly available codecs.
Desktop composition redirection	Enabled	To allow rendering of WDM-generated graphics on clients.
Desktop composition redirection quality	Medium	Sets default compression for desktop composition redirection.

These are some of the key changes that were introduced in XenDesktop 7.x and everyone should be aware of these before playing with HDX policies.

When we open HDX Monitor with the default graphics settings enabled, we notice that the Adaptive Display is disabled:

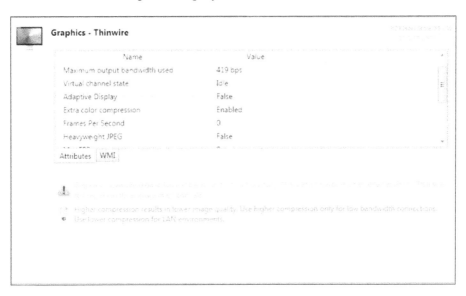

This means that you are using new codecs that are available with XenDesktop 7.x and not using first generation Adaptive Display.

If you look at the **WMI** tab for advance details, you will notice that the legacy graphics mode is turned off by a policy:

This is now default behavior. If you have your user based in LAN environments and you want to revert back to the Adaptive Display mode, you can always change the policy to enable the legacy graphics mode, which in turn would enable first generation Adaptive Display. Moreover, you need to switch off the desktop composition redirection to make it work.

However, keep in mind that changing the graphic settings to Adaptive Display can badly impact your WAN-based mobile users.

 To provide HDX experience to users working on graphics-intensive applications, you can leverage GPU rendering on physical devices in the data center or GPU rendering on the hypervisor using GPU passthrough. For more details, please refer to the following links:

- `www.nvidia.com/object/xendesktop-vgpu.html`
- `https://www.citrix.com/content/dam/citrix/en_us/documents/go/configuring-xenserver-to-use-nvidia-grid.pdf?accessmode=direct`
- `https://www.citrix.com/content/dam/citrix/en_us/documents/go/reviewers-guide-remote-3d-graphics-apps-part-2-vsphere-gpu-passthrough.pdf`

- **Graphics - Thinwire Advanced**: This is used to monitor the bandwidth of the graphics in a particular session; it can also be used to monitor network performance.

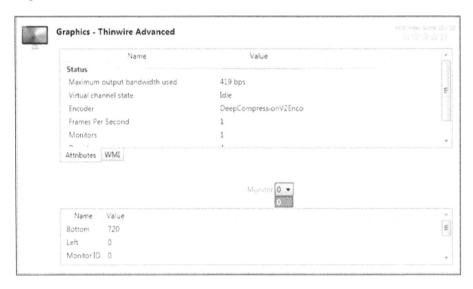

- **Mapped Client Drives**: This component is used to validate the client drive mapping functionality:

- **Network**: This component is used to monitor the network bandwidth performance for established sessions:

Sometimes, you will notice an error on the network component saying *Citrix Receiver does not support collecting network information.*

This error is reported due to inactive ICA sessions. You should make sure that the session you are monitoring is active. The other reason could be that the Perfmon counters are corrupted.

- **Printing** and **Scanner**: These tell you whether your printers' and scanners' redirection is working fine or not. The following screenshot shows the settings for scanners:

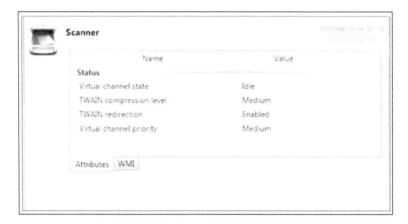

The following screenshot shows the settings for printers.

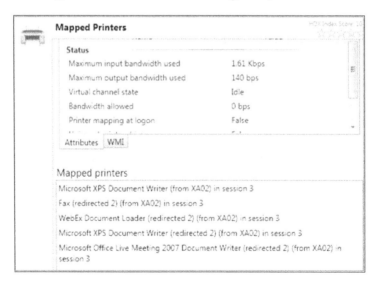

- **Smart Cards**: If you use smart cards in your environment, you can get the diagnostic details here:

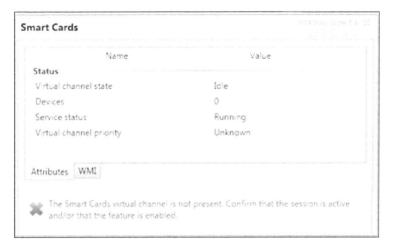

- **System Information**: This provides the system information for the XenApp server or the VDA device that you are monitoring:

- **VDA**: This provides the details related to the VDA agent:

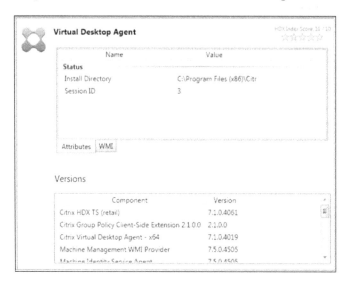

- **Windows Media**: Monitoring this component can help you with Windows Media redirection issues in your XenApp or XenDesktop environment:

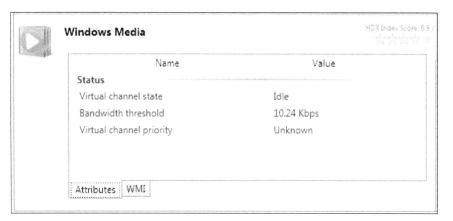

 To understand Windows Media redirection, you can refer to the Citrix article at http://support.citrix.com/article/CTX137469.

Citrix Scout

In the recent past, Citrix released a tool called Citrix Scout; it collects diagnostic information for the XenDesktop product suite. It has been made user-friendly and now has just a start and stop button to capture a diagnostic log.

You can download Citrix Scout from `http://support.citrix.com/article/` `CTX130147`.

 For XenApp/XenDesktop 7.5 and above, you need not download this tool. Scout is preinstalled on all the controller servers.

You can upload the Scout log to the Citrix Auto Support site (TAAS) to get a quick analysis by the TAAS engines.

There are certain prerequisites that should be met before you start configuring Citrix Scout; they are as follows:

- Local admin rights on the Delivery Controller server
- Local admin rights on the remote machines
- WinRM needs to be enabled and configured on remote machines
- Remote registry needs to be enabled on remote machines
- All machines should be in the same domain
- You should be running at least PowerShell version 2.0
- File and print services should be enabled on remote machines
- .NET framework 3.5 SP1 and above

Configuring and running Citrix Scout

Before we jump into configuring Scout, let's have a look at the basic configuration of Citrix Scout. Launch the Citrix Scout console and then click on **Config** | **Settings** in the main menu.

The basic configuration enables you to change the settings for CDF tracing within this tool:

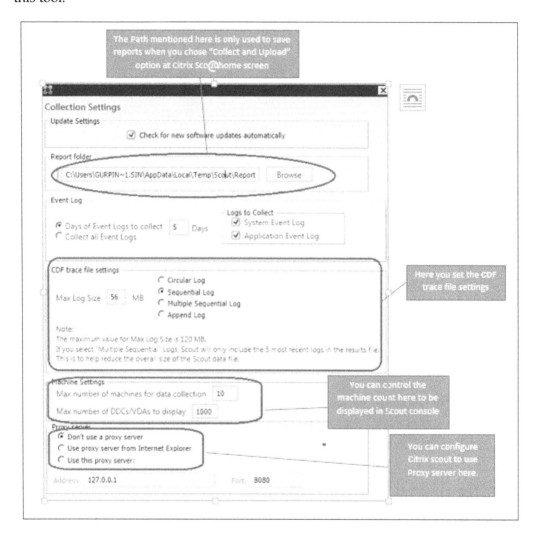

If you look at the utilities included within this tool, you will notice that CDFControl is one, along with XDPing and XDDBDiag:

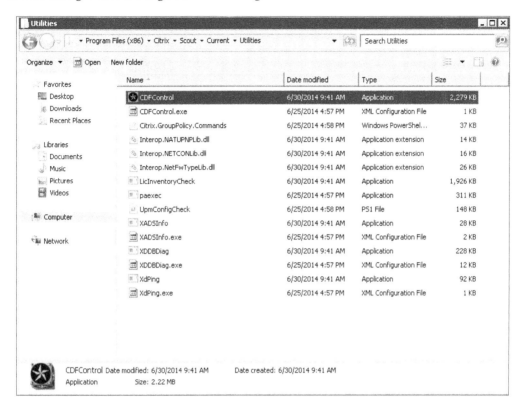

These utilities can be used as standalone utilities to perform diagnosis. Citrix Scout uses CDFControl to perform CDF tracing.

The following steps need to be followed when configuring Citrix Scout for the first time on the Controller server prior to XenDesktop v7.x:

1. Download and unzip the package on the Controller server.
2. Execute `run.exe`.
3. From the **Tool** menu, click on **Options** and select **Config**.
4. Make changes to the default settings, if required.
5. Click on **Start CDF Trace**.
6. Select all controllers or VDAs experiencing the issue.
7. Select the default modules to start the trace.
8. Reproduce the issue for which you would like to capture details.
9. Click **Stop CDF Trace** once the issue has been reproduced.

CDF trace files are written to the same folder where you have downloaded Scout.

Let's have a look at capturing a basic CDF trace. To start the CDF trace, you need to click on **Start CDF Trace** within the Citrix Scout console. You will notice that the Delivery Controller from where you started the trace is automatically selected, as shown in the following screenshot:

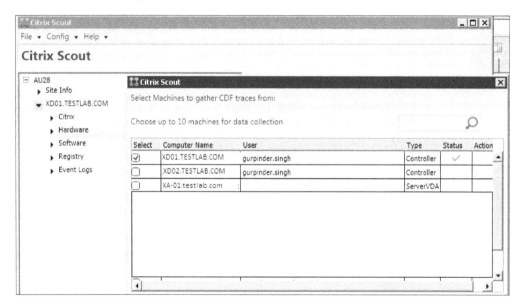

If you have any issues or if the previously mentioned prerequisites are not met, you will see an action item under the **Action** column:

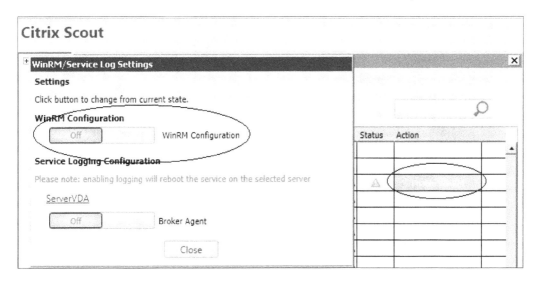

In the preceding screenshot, it is clearly visible that the particular VDA machine doesn't have WinRM enabled on it. You can double-click on the action item and it will give you an option to enable WinRM remotely, provided that you have admin privileges on the remote machine.

To enable WinRM manually on each machine, you can launch the PowerShell CLI with administrative privileges on specific machines and type the following command:

```
winrm qc
```

This is shown in the following screenshot:

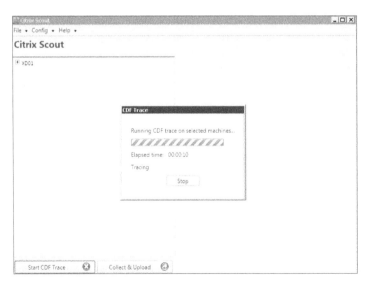

There can be instances where a firewall exists between the controller and other VDAs; in that case, we need to make sure that the firewall is configured to allow communication on WinRM port 5985.

Once we are done resolving these action items, we will be good to proceed with CDF tracing. You can click on **Continue** to proceed with your CDF trace as shown in the following screenshot:

Citrix Scout uses CDFControl in the background; it actually copies the executable to the remote machine and executes it remotely to capture the data. Once the trace is stopped, the executable is deleted from the remote machine and the data is copied to the controller from where the Citrix Scout is running.

We have already understood in a previous section of this chapter how CDF works to capture data and how we can parse the data to read logs. For detailed information on how to use Citrix Scout, please watch the Citrix TV video at `http://www.citrix.com/tv/#videos/9268`.

Citrix Quick Launch

The Citrix Quick Launch tool is used to create ICA sessions similar to the older ICA clients. However, it is not a replacement for your Citrix ICA client or receiver. It doesn't work until you have the ICA client installed on the client device.

It was solely developed by Citrix to be used by administrators to test and is not recommended or supported by Citrix. It can be your go-to tool if you are troubleshooting published application launch issues. With this tool, you can create ICA files with specified XML service port details and the right launch mechanism:

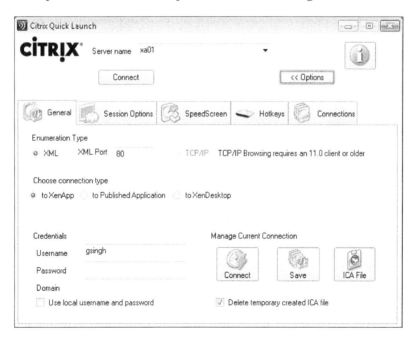

To download and configure it correctly for the purpose of using it with XenDesktop-and XenApp-based ICA sessions, please read the article at `http://support.citrix.com/article/CTX122536`.

 This tool has limitations with XenDesktop 7.x, as Citrix has deprecated the creation of ICA files with the release of the XenDesktop 7.x.

Print Detective

Print Detective is a utility used to troubleshoot issues related to printer drivers. It gathers information related to all the printer drivers, including driver-specific information, and then enumerates them on the specified Windows machine.

It is one of the most important tools to troubleshoot printer issues in the XenApp and XenDesktop environment. The tool is really useful to remove or delete conflicting printer drivers that can make your XenApp server or user VDI machine unstable and can cause the **print spooler** service to keep crashing.

You can launch it by executing `PrintDetective.exe` to gather information on the relevant print drivers, as shown in the following screenshot:

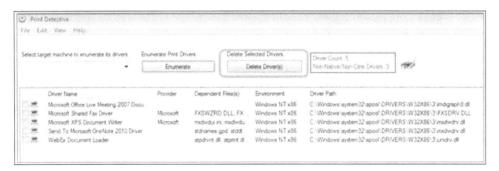

You can analyze your event viewer application log to get the details of bad printer drivers that are crashing the print spooler service on the XenApp server or VDI:

After you identify the respective print drivers, you can delete them using the Print Detective tool from the specific Windows machine.

As a best practice, you should configure Citrix universal printing in your environment, unless there is a specific requirement from your customer to allow the installation of native printer drivers.

This tool can be downloaded from `http://support.citrix.com/article/CTX116474`.

StressPrinters

The StressPrinters utility is used to troubleshoot printer problems in a terminal service or remote desktop service environment and is basically meant for Citrix XenApp. However, you can also use it for standalone Windows operating system and XenDesktop VDIs, as it doesn't have any dependency on Citrix-specific components.

This tool is used to simulate the creation of printers using specific printer drivers. This helps in identifying the corrupted or conflicting printer drivers that are actually causing the spooler to crash.

In a remote desktop service environment (Citrix XenApp), multiple users log in to work on published applications or desktops. Some drivers don't respond properly when processing multiple threads of printing jobs in a remote desktop service environment. Due to this, the print spooler sometimes crashes. This utility can help reproduce the issue in a simulated StressPrinters GUI environment using the same printer driver.

You can download this utility from `http://support.citrix.com/article/CTX109374`.

Using StressPrinters

Once you have downloaded the utility, unzip it in the folder on the XenApp server or VDI machine where all the printer drivers are installed to map specific printers:

1. Select the appropriate `StressPrinters.exe` setup as per your operating system (x86 or x64) to launch the utility:

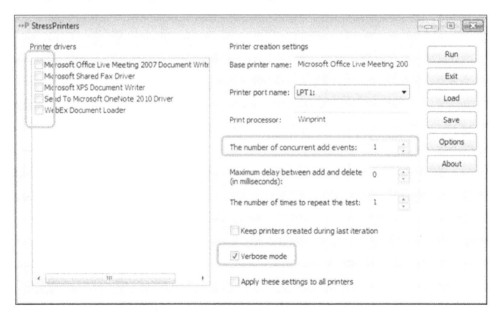

2. Select the print drivers that you want to run the **stress test** for and then select the number of concurrent add events to set how often the printer should be created.

   You should select at least 5 add events for a valid stress test.

 To know the details of each parameter, refer to the Citrix article at http://support.citrix.com/article/CTX109374.

3. To start your stress test, click on the **Run** button and you will get an output similar to the following screenshot:

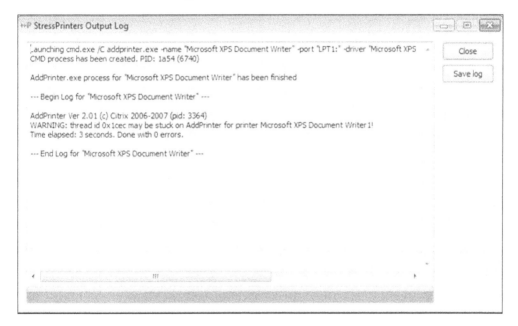

You should have noticed that the stress test for the Microsoft XPS document printer has finished successfully and doesn't show any errors. However, you will see the following error while running the test against a problematic driver, which may crash the spooler service:

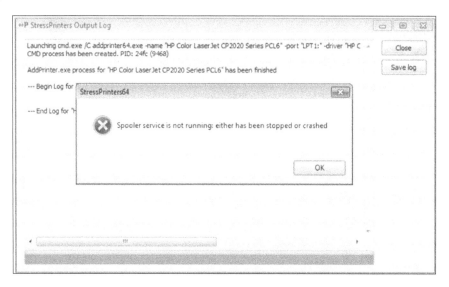

XenDesktop® Site Checker

The XenDesktop Site Checker tool is used to validate the functioning of active XenDesktop sites. It enumerates the XenDesktop site brokers, services, hosts, assignments, catalogs, provisioning tasks, and schemas with the user of the PowerShell SDKs in the background.

You can use this tool to check the status of services, whether they are running OK or not; service instances are registered and it even provides the ability to enable logging for each service. However, this tool is outdated and can be used only for XenDesktop 5.x sites. A new tool is under development to replace this tool for XenDesktop 7.x sites.

To download and learn more about this tool, which is to be used on XenDesktop 5.x sites, you can refer to the Citrix article at http://support.citrix.com/article/CTX133767.

The development release of the tool for XenDesktop 7.x sites is available at https://www.dropbox.com/s/q3xrx9c3znri6kl/XDSiteDiag.zip.

The new tool is not supported by Citrix yet, but it can provide you with similar functionality to help you troubleshoot your XenDesktop 7.x site issues. You need to have administrative privileges on the XenDesktop site to run this tool.

It provides a similar interface as Citrix Studio with some improved features. Let's have a look at the GUI interface of the tool launched for the XA/XD 7.5 site:

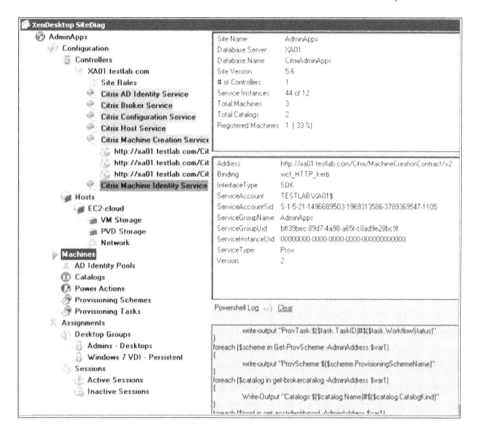

It provides the following advanced features that the Citrix Studio doesn't have and can also help you troubleshoot issues beyond Citrix Studio:

- Ability to provide XenDesktop site services status to check and fix issues
- Service logging option for each service on every controller server
- Option to delete VM and PVD storage
- Control over power actions

- Edit advance desktop settings to manage idle pool settings, logoff behavior, the *WillShutdownAfterUse* option, and more

- All object details in a tree view: AD Identity pools, provisioning schemas, and many more.

- Sessions details

- Search elements in a site

You can download the tool to get it tested against your test environment and to explore the enhanced features it provides. We have to wait for a final version to be released by Citrix officially, with support for XenDesktop 7.x sites.

XDPing

XDPing is a command-line tool developed by Citrix to assist in analyzing and troubleshooting misconfiguration issues in the XenDesktop environment. You can run this tool from the PowerShell prompt on a remote computer or from the Controller server; it provides information about all your network interfaces, logged-in users, time synchronization issues, and domain membership details along with DNS lookup data.

This tool is supported on all the latest releases of the XenDesktop product. The tool comes with two files: XDping.exe and XDPing.exe.config. You can place these two files wherever you want. To run this tool from the command prompt, you can browse to the directory where it is placed and then run the following command to learn about all the available syntaxes it provides:

```
C:\Xdping /help
```

Running this tool with the /host switch will give you the following output; this can help administrators troubleshoot any communication issues between a controller and VDA machines:

```
XDPing 2.3.0.0

Created by Citrix Systems Engineering and Escalation teams.

Help us improve this tool by providing feedback through http://twitter.com/CitrixEscEMEA.


UpdateVersion Error The remote server returned an error: (407) Proxy Authentication Required.
```

```
Checking version : You are using the latest version.


---------------------------------------------------------------------
Local Machine::


  NetBIOS Name = XD01.testlab.com

  OS Version   = Microsoft Windows NT 6.2.9200.0

  Platform     = X64 Platform


  Computer Domain: TESTLAB.com

    Role       = Member Server

    Membership = VerifTESTLABd, SID
:S-1-5-21-962264046-888720465-393826521-76512 [OK]


---------------------------------------------------------------------
User::


  User Name      = Gurpinder.singh

  User Domain    = TESTLAB

  Authentication = Kerberos [OK]

  Groups:

     TESTLAB\Domain Users

     Everyone

     BUILTIN\Administrators

     BUILTIN\Users

     BUILTIN\Remote Desktop Users

     NT AUTHORITY\INTERACTIVE

     CONSOLE LOGON

     NT AUTHORITY\Authenticated Users

     NT AUTHORITY\This Organization

     LOCAL

     TESTLAB\Citrix-Admin

     TESTLAB\TESTLAB_VDI_Access_Group
```

```
         Authentication authority asserted identity


  ----------------------------------------------------------------
Local Machine Time::


  UTC   = 26/08/2015 10:48:27 AM

  Local = 26/08/2015 8:48:27 PM (AUS Eastern Standard Time)

  DST   = No

  NtpServer = time.windows.com,0x9


  ----------------------------------------------------------------
Domain Controller(s) Time::



Date/Time from TESTLAB.com : 26/08/2015 8:48:27 PM : Time difference
(mins): 0 [OK]


  ----------------------------------------------------------------
Network Interfaces::


  NIC #0 "Ethernet":
    Network       = Ethernet, 10Gb/s, Up
    MAC           = D0:50:56:D2:2D:3D
    DNS suffix    = TESTLAB.com
    DNS servers   = 192.168.215.11 192.168.227.1
    WINS servers  = 192.168.227.1 192.168.215.11
    Gateways      = 192.168.206.254
    DHCP server   = 192.168.227.201
    Address #0    = fe80::1c8f:eac3:b3e6:9c4b%12/0.0.0.0, Preferred,
Origin=WellKnown/LinkLayerAddress
         Lease = 91173/4294967295/4294967295
    Address #1    = 192.168.206.214/255.255.255.0, Preferred, Origin=Dhcp/
OriginDhcp
         Lease = 691406/600250/600250
```

```
  NIC #1 "Loopback Pseudo-Interface 1", Loopback:

    Network      = Loopback, 1073Mb/s, Up

    DNS servers  = fec0:0:0:ffff::1%1 fec0:0:0:ffff::2%1
fec0:0:0:ffff::3%1

    Address #0   = ::1/0.0.0.0, Preferred, Origin=WellKnown/WellKnown

          Lease = 91183/4294967295/4294967295

    Address #1   = 127.0.0.1/255.0.0.0, Preferred, Origin=WellKnown/
WellKnown

          Lease = 91183/4294967295/4294967295


  NIC #2 "isatap.TESTLAB.com":

    Network      = Tunnel, 0Gb/s, Down

    MAC          = 00:00:00:00:00:00:00:E0


  NIC #3 "6TO4 Adapter":

    Network      = Tunnel, 3Gb/s, Up

    MAC          = 00:00:00:00:00:00:00:E0

    DNS suffix   = TESTLAB.com

    DNS servers  = 192.168.215.11 192.168.227.1

    Address #0   = 2002:94c3:ced6::94c3:ced6/0.0.0.0, Preferred,
Origin=WellKnown/WellKnown

          Lease = 91109/4294967295/4294967295


---------------------------------------------------------------------

WCF Endpoints: CitrixBrokerService::

C:\Program Files\Citrix\Broker\Service\BrokerService.exe

Version Number :7.6.0.5024


XenDesktop version 7.6.0.5024

 wsHttpBinding:

 Citrix.Broker.Admin.SDK.IBrokerAdminService:

 http://localhost/Citrix/BrokerAdminService/v2:

    Ping Service: /Citrix/BrokerAdminService/v2

      Connect = Tcp to [::1]:80 via ::1 ("Loopback Pseudo-Interface 1")
[OK]
```

```
        Service = Listening [OK]
  wsHttpBinding:
  Citrix.Broker.Admin.IBrokerAdminQuery:
  http://localhost/Citrix/BrokerAdminQuery/v1:
     Ping Service: /Citrix/BrokerAdminQuery/v1
        Connect = Tcp to [::1]:80 via ::1 ("Loopback Pseudo-Interface 1")
[OK]
        Service = Listening [OK]
  wsHttpBinding:
  Citrix.EnvTest.Interfaces.TESTLABnvTestApi:
  http://localhost/Citrix/BrokerEnvTests/v1:
     Ping Service: /Citrix/BrokerEnvTests/v1
        Connect = Tcp to [::1]:80 via ::1 ("Loopback Pseudo-Interface 1")
[OK]
        Service = Listening [OK]
  wsHttpBinding:
  Citrix.Cds.Protocol.Controller.IRegistrar:
  http://localhost/Citrix/CdsController/IRegistrar:
     Ping Service: /Citrix/CdsController/IRegistrar
        Connect = Tcp to [::1]:80 via ::1 ("Loopback Pseudo-Interface 1")
[OK]
        Service = Listening [OK]
  wsHttpBinding:
  Citrix.Cds.Protocol.Controller.ITicketing:
  http://localhost/Citrix/CdsController/ITicketing:
     Ping Service: /Citrix/CdsController/ITicketing
        Connect = Tcp to [::1]:80 via ::1 ("Loopback Pseudo-Interface 1")
[OK]
        Service = Listening [OK]
  wsHttpBinding:
  Citrix.Cds.Protocol.Controller.IDynamicDataSink:
  http://localhost/Citrix/CdsController/IDynamicDataSink:
     Ping Service: /Citrix/CdsController/IDynamicDataSink
        Connect = Tcp to [::1]:80 via ::1 ("Loopback Pseudo-Interface 1")
[OK]
        Service = Listening [OK]
  wsHttpBinding:
```

```
Citrix.Cds.Protocol.Controller.INotifyBroker:

http://localhost/Citrix/CdsController/INotifyBroker:

    Ping Service: /Citrix/CdsController/INotifyBroker

      Connect = Tcp to [::1]:80 via ::1 ("Loopback Pseudo-Interface 1")
[OK]

      Service = Listening [OK]



----------------------------------------------------------------

Controller Services::


  Service  : Licensing services not present [OK]


----------------------------------------------------------------

DNS Lookups for Local Machine::


  Host Name  : XD01.testlab.com

  Address #0 = fe80::1c8f:eac3:b3e6:9c4b%12 (rDNS: XD01.testlab.com.
TESTLAB.com) [OK]

  Address #1 = 192.168.206.214 (rDNS: XD01.testlab.com.TESTLAB.com) [OK]

  Address #2 = 2002:94c3:ced6::94c3:ced6 (rDNS: XD01.testlab.com) [OK]


----------------------------------------------------------------

Event Log Check::
```

 For more information on this tool's usage and its download instructions, please read the article at http://support.citrix.com/article/CTX123278.

XDDBDiag

XDDBDiag is a command line tool provided by Citrix to help us perform consistency checks on data and connectivity verification for the XenDesktop site database. It provides diagnostic output in comma-separated value files (.csv).

The output files contain the following information:

- Site information
- Virtual Desktop Agent information
- Current connections/connection log
- Hypervisor connections
- Policy information
- Desktop groups
- Controller information
- Database information

The tool can be run from a command prompt on the controller. The syntax to be used to run this tool is as follows:

```
C:\XDDBDiag windows MySQLServer SQLDB
```

The result of the preceding command is as follows:

```
Data Compression disabled

windowscitrixdbXD_test_dbXDDBDiag 4 Citrix Support

UpdateVersion Error The remote server returned an error: (407) Proxy
Authentication Required.

Unable to detect latest version - Can not find https://taas.citrix.com/
tools/XDDbDiag/version.xml

Preparing to execute database consistency checks...

DBCollation ->Latin1_General_100_CI_AS_KS

Schema Version Detected = 7.6.0.0

XDDBCheck.sql: Revision Excalibur


SQL Server summary (on citrixdb):
  Microsoft SQL Server 2008 R2 (SP2) - 10.50.4000.0 (X64)
      Jun 28 2012 08:36:30
      Copyright (c) Microsoft Corporation
      Standard Edition (64-bit) on Windows NT 6.0 <X64> (Build 6002:
Service Pack 2) (Hypervisor)


Database:
```

```
XD_test_db
Aug 26 2015 11:15AM (UTC)


XenDesktop Site summary:
  Schema version: ................ 7.6.0.0
  # Controllers ................. 1
    1: S-1-5-21-962264046-888720465-393826521-76512, [TESTLAB\XD01],
7.6.0.5024, Active
  # Catalogs .................... 1
    3: [XD POC], SingleImage, Random (Shared)
  # Desktop Groups .............. 1
    1: [XD VDI TEST], Shared, Enabled
  # Access Policy rules ......... 2
    1: [XD VDI TEST_Direct], DISABLED
    2: [XD VDI TEST_AG], Enabled
  # Entitlement Policy rules ..... 1
    1: [XD VDI TEST_1], DesktopGroup=1, Enabled
  # Assignment Policy rules ...... 0
  # Hypervisor Connections ....... 0
  # Configured machines ......... 3
  # Registered machines ......... 3 (0 soft-registered)
  # Established sessions ........ 1 (0 non-brokered/disconnected)
  # Establishing sessions ....... 0


Running consistency checks...


*** Warning: 3 machines with inconsistent catalog/hypervisor connection
data.


==>  1 problems found.


Controller Database Connection settings
```

```
Controller,Server=citrixdb;Initial Catalog=XD_test_db;Integrated
Security=True,Passed

ADIdentitySchema,Server=citrixdb;Initial Catalog=XD_test_db;Integrated
Security=True - Passed

Analytics,Server=citrixdb;Initial Catalog=XD_test_db;Integrated
Security=True - Passed

ConfigLoggingSiteSchema,Server=citrixdb;Initial Catalog=XD_test_
db;Integrated Security=True - Passed

ConfigurationSchema,Server=citrixdb;Initial Catalog=XD_test_db;Integrated
Security=True - Passed

DAS,Server=citrixdb;Initial Catalog=XD_test_db;Integrated Security=True -
Passed

DesktopUpdateManagerSchema,Server=citrixdb;Initial Catalog=XD_test_
db;Integrated Security=True - Passed

EnvTestServiceSchema,Server=citrixdb;Initial Catalog=XD_test_
db;Integrated Security=True - Passed

HostingUnitServiceSchema,Server=citrixdb;Initial Catalog=XD_test_
db;Integrated Security=True - Passed

Monitor,Server=citrixdb;Initial Catalog=XD_test_db;Integrated
Security=True - Passed

StorefrontSchema,Server=citrixdb;Initial Catalog=XD_test_db;Integrated
Security=True - Passed
```

```
Exporting Data...

Export Completed...
```

 To download usage details, please read the Citrix article at `http://support.citrix.com/article/` `CTX128075#prodrelated`.

Xperf or Windows Performance Recorder

In the past few years, many administrators have relied on the so called **Xperf** tool for troubleshooting all kinds of performance issues, including slow logons. This tool has gained popularity for its ability to provide graphical analysis, stack tracing, process lifetime details, and so on.

Due to its popularity, it was supposed to become a mainstream tool for all Windows administrators. However, Microsoft soon released a tool called **Windows Performance Recorder** to replace Xperf.

The decision taken by Microsoft to rename and release a better and easy-to-configure tool was due to the fact that obtaining traces with Xperf was at times complex and required administrators to work hard to correctly configure it using stack-wise flags.

Microsoft released Windows Performance Recorder, where they have created a UI that looks quite easy to configure and has made the life of a Windows administrator easy.

It is available as a part of the Windows SDK kit for Windows 8 but it works on the Windows 7 and Windows 2008 R2 platforms as well. You can download it from `http://www.microsoft.com/en-us/download/details.aspx?id=30652`.

Using Windows Performance Recorder (WPR)

After downloading the Windows SDK kit for Windows 8, run the setup to install the Windows Performance Toolkit on your Windows machine. Refer to the following screenshot; as we are installing **Windows Performance Toolkit**, you can deselect all the other options:

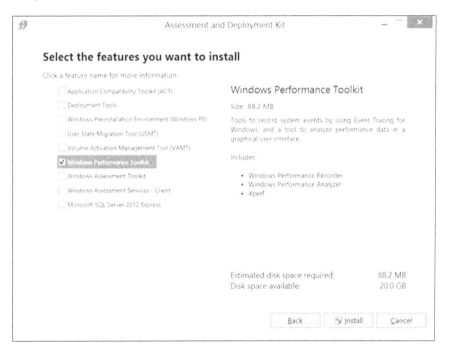

By default, the WPR kit is installed in the path: `C:\Program Files (x86)\Windows Kits\Windows Performance Toolkit`. You have the option to install it on alternate machines by using the redistributable package under `C:\Program Files (x86)\Windows Kits\Windows Performance Toolkit\Redistributables`:

 Microsoft also provides redistributables for Windows ARM, which is a plus point as it allows you to configure toolkit on tablets and notebooks running Windows RT.

Once you have installed the Windows Performance Toolkit, you will get the following three options in the Start menu:

- **Windows Performance Recorder**: To set and start your trace
- **Windows Performance Analyzer**: To analyze the trace
- **GPU View**: To analyze the trace in GPU mode

To start your first trace, you require administrative privileges on the Windows machine; you might see a UAC prompt on your computer screen while running the WPR. If you are running the 64-bit version of an operating system, you need to disable the paging executive to successfully collect event traces.

To achieve this, you can either do it via the command prompt by issuing the `wpr.exe -disablepagingexecutive on` command, or while running the setup for the first time, it will prompt you to disable the paging executive, click on **OK** to proceed. It will require the machine to be restarted. Make sure you turn it back off when you are done with your trace, as it can affect performance adversely.

When you run the WPR GUI for the first time you will see the following screen:

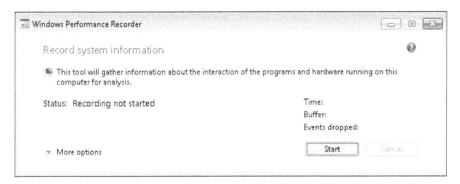

When you click on **Start**, it will fire your trace and load the default general profile for your trace. A general profile is used to record all default traces with recordings of basic system issues and performance data. The general profile uses the **NT Kernel Logger** collector and **WPR_initiated_WPR Event Collector**. Let's have a look at the following screenshot to inspect the event tracing data collectors set in Perfmon when the trace is running:

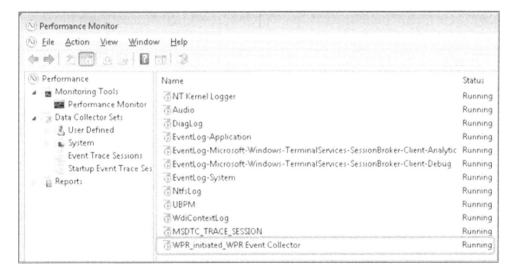

Once the trace capture is running, the WPR GUI will look like the following screenshot:

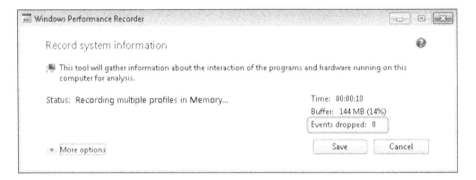

You may have noticed that **Events dropped** is highlighted. This is important; if you have numerous events dropped; you may discard the running trace and start a fresh capture. Dropped events lead to an indecisive analysis.

You can click on **Save** to save your trace in the directory specified by you. By default, it will save the trace file in the Documents\WPR directory of the user running the trace; this is due to security concerns. You can click on **Cancel** to stop the trace:

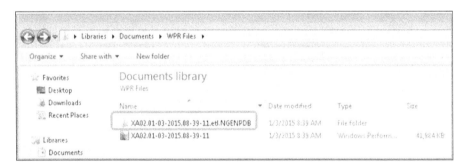

The file is saved in the machinname.date.time format; along with this file, you will also have one folder ending with NGENPDB. This folder contains the PDBs that are required to diagnose issues with the managed components.

PDB, or **Program Database**, is a proprietary file format (developed by Microsoft) that stores debugging information about a program (or, commonly, program modules such as a DLL or EXE). PDB files commonly have a .pdb extension.

We have gained a basic understanding of the WPR tool and also how to run a basic trace with it. It's time to proceed with capturing a trace configured with advanced options.

Advanced recording

To record an advanced trace, you need to expand the options of the WPR GUI and select the required advanced options, as shown in the following screenshot:

These are the advanced options that are provided with WPR recording; it will increase the overhead of your trace and also the size of your trace file. Always make sure to check only those options that are required and never check all checkboxes. Take a note of the **Performance scenario** drop-down; it will help you choose scenario-based options to troubleshoot your issues:

- **General**: It is used to record the general performance of the running computer

- **Boot**: Helps in recording performance while the computer is booting

- **Shutdown**: Helps in recording performance while shutting down the computer

- **Reboot Cycle**: Helps in recording performance during the reboot cycle

- **Standby/Resume**: Helps in recording performance when switching the computer from standby to the resume state

- **Hibernate/Resume**: Helps in recording performance when switching the computer from hibernation to the resume state

The **Detail level** dropdown gives you an option to select **Verbose** logging, which is the default, or **Light** if you do not want to capture every bit of data. The **Logging mode** dropdown is set to **Memory** for a general performance scenario; we should leave this setting to the default option that is being recommended as per the performance scenario.

> For the **Performance scenario** options chosen — **Boot**, **Shutdown**, **Reboot cycle**, **Standby/resume**, and **Hibernate/resume** — WPR will by default choose to log a file. This cannot be changed in the GUI.

You can create custom profiles that can be used to capture WPR traces. Please refer to the MSDN article at `http://msdn.microsoft.com/en-us/library/windows/desktop/hh162947.aspx`.

Reading a trace

You can start reading your trace file by opening it in Windows Performance Analyzer. The trace will display system, storage, compute, and memory activities in a graphical explorer.

You can right-click on each activity to add it and start analyzing the data:

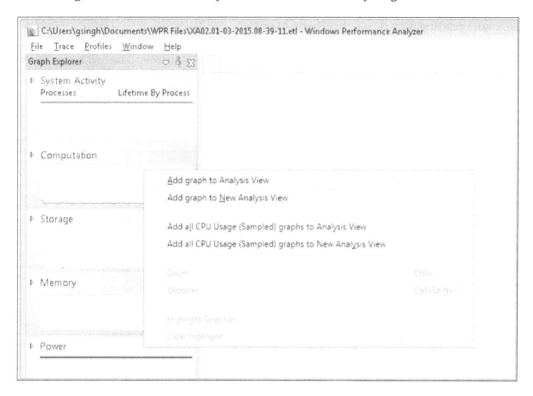

Before starting, we need to make sure that the symbol files are loaded in the console. Please go to **Menu** and click on the **Trace** dropdown to select **Configure symbols**. It should automatically have the symbol path configured to the MSDN site and `SRV*C:\Users\username\Documents\WPR Files\filename.etl.NGENPDB`. Click on **Load symbols** to get the symbols loaded on the console. You need to have an Internet connection to load symbols from the MSDN site.

We will now study one random trace taken during a normal user logon event for a XenDesktop user. The logon was very fast and took fewer than 20 seconds. Let's start reading a trace for this logon event:

Interestingly, we can see a lot of spikes on the **Computation**, **Storage**, and **Memory** graphs. Let's examine the graphs one by one, starting with the **System Activity** graph.

The System Activity graph

When you see the following System Activity graph, you can note the time duration that each process took for a logon event; the details also provide the start-time and end-time for each process. The duration for some processes is shown in red, which denotes that the duration is longer than the expected time for the given processes. This is shown in the following screenshot:

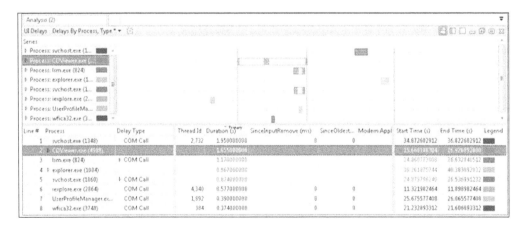

You can expand particular processes to see more details and you can also filter to see details of a particular process to analyze it.

The Computation graph

The following graph looks really scary, doesn't it?

In this graph, at the top left, the utilization is sorted on the basis of utilization by process. You can toggle this switch by selecting other options such as utilization by CPU, utilization by process and thread, and so on. You can move the cursor to the individual CPU lines to know the underlying process of utilization:

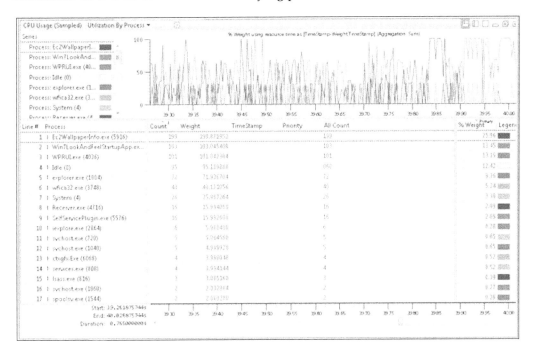

The graph indicates several processes and their utilization during the logon event. This is normal as during the logon event, many processes fire up and create CPU spikes but, later on, CPU utilization comes down as the logon is processed. We need to analyze the data and spend time in identifying the processes causing the delay, if the logon is delayed. However, in our case, we know that the logon took just under 20 seconds and it is not a matter of concern.

The Storage graph

In the following graph, you can see that the utilization is sorted by disk. It shows that disk I/O has spiked during a fraction of 9-10 seconds. You can identify the processes and file system activities that have caused the spikes. You can also toggle the utilization switch to select options as shown in the dropdown menu, to perform a more effective analysis per process or I/O activity.

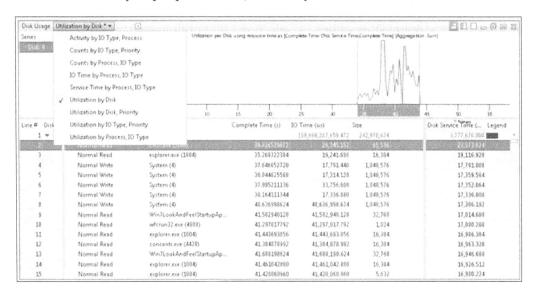

The Memory graph

The Memory graph provides details about memory utilization by given categories; have a look at the following graph for details:

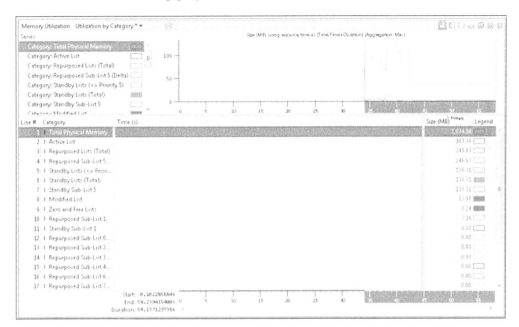

To get started with WPA, we recommend that you watch Microsoft's *Introduction to the new WPA user interface* video at `http://channel9.msdn.com/Events/Build/BUILD2011/HW-926P`.

Wireshark

If you are working as a Citrix administrator, you may have heard users complaining about slowness and sessions dropping out for published applications and Citrix desktops. Sometimes, it becomes really difficult to identify the root cause of slowness.

Wireshark is a wonderful tool to troubleshoot slow network problems. You can download Wireshark from `http://www.wireshark.org/download.html`.

 There are other tools in the market that you can use to perform a similar level of troubleshooting. One is Microsoft Netmon. I personally like Wireshark for troubleshooting issues.

Install the tool with the default options and proceed with opening the Wireshark console for the first time. The GUI interface looks as shown in the following screenshot:

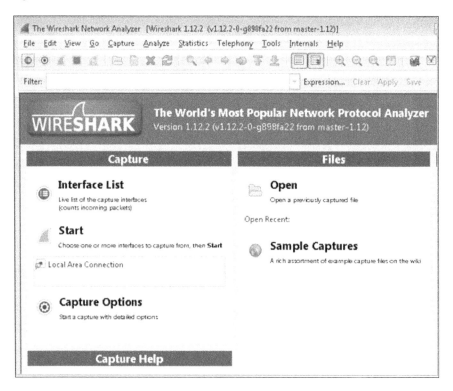

You need to select a network interface to start a capture. To select an interface, click on **Interface List** and start the capture for the selected interface by clicking on **Start**:

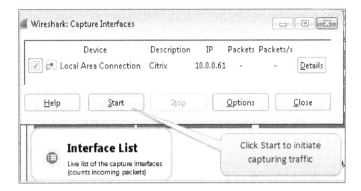

The trace window is displayed in three views:

- **View 1**: This shows the packet list and summary of each packet information
- **View 2**: You can select the packet and expand it to explore the packet details here
- **View 3**: This shows the raw packet bytes

These are shown in the following screenshot:

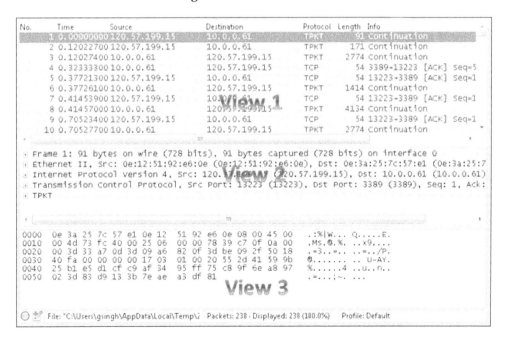

You can customize the view and toggle the options to turn it on/off. The **Time** column is the most important column and we should customize the precision up to milliseconds. Also, don't forget to enable the Delta time, as shown in the following screenshot:

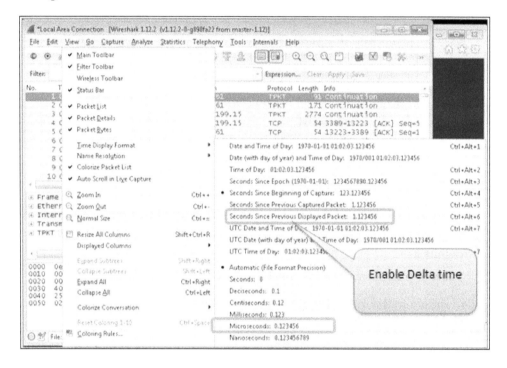

Now, we are ready to analyze the HTTP/S traffic for our Citrix XenDesktop URL to identify any slowness or network drops.

We started capturing the trace on Wireshark, opened the web browser on a client `XA02.testlab.com` server, and browsed to `http://xa01/citrix/storeweb`, which is our StoreFront URL for launching Notepad applications.

While analyzing traffic, we observed that the DNS query took ~20ms to resolve the destination XA01 server where our StoreFront URL is hosted:

After DNS resolution, the client will send a connection request to the StoreFront server. This will be the first TCP SYN packet in the TCP three-way handshake. Now, to isolate this connection, we need to use a TCP stream filter. To enable a TCP stream filter, right-click on any packet in the TCP connection and select **TCP Stream Filter**.

We need to isolate this connection to compare the network roundtrip time to the server response time. After applying the TCP stream filter, we will be able to analyze the client-to-server response time:

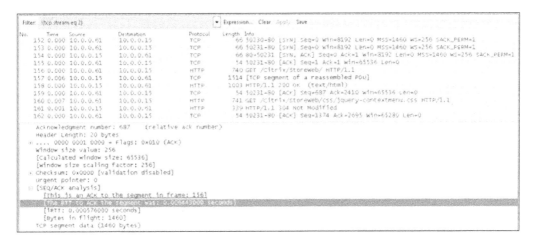

With the preceding analysis, we can conclude that the RTT time-to-server response time is less than 7 milliseconds, which is a very good response rate. Similarly, we can identify the time taken to launch the application by filtering HTTP traffic. This can help us in diagnosing slowness issues on Citrix XenApp/XenDesktop farms.

> To learn more about Wireshark, you can read *Network Analysis Using Wireshark Cookbook, Yoram Orzach, Packt Publishing*. The book is available at https://www.packtpub.com/networking-and-servers/network-analysis-using-wireshark-cookbook.

The PowerShell SDK for XenDesktop®

Every Citrix administrator working on the XenDesktop environment must be adept at working with PowerShell **cmdlets** to query and troubleshoot a XenDesktop environment. Citrix provides the PowerShell SDK that interacts with Desktop Studio to perform administrative actions using the .NET framework.

Before we start with the PowerShell SDK for XenDesktop, we should set up and configure a PoSH profile.

What is a PoSH profile?

A PoSH profile is a customized PowerShell script that sets your PoSH environment once you fire up PowerShell on the XenDesktop Controller server. It can contain cmdlets, scripts, functions, or any PowerShell commands.

To configure a PoSH profile, you need to launch the PowerShell administrative shell and type the following command:

```
New-item -type file $profile
```

You might be surprised to see the following error on the screen:

```
PS C:\Windows\system32> New-item -type file $profile
New-item : Could not find a part of the path
'C:\Users\gsingh\Documents\WindowsPowerShell\Microsoft.PowerShell_profile.ps1'.
At line:1 char:1
+ New-item -type file $profile
+ ~~~~~~~~~~~~~~~~~~~~~~~~~~~~~~
    + CategoryInfo          : WriteError: (C:\Users\gsingh...ell_profile.ps1:String) [New-Item], DirectoryNotFoundExce
   ption
    + FullyQualifiedErrorId : NewItemIOError,Microsoft.PowerShell.Commands.NewItemCommand
```

If you look at the error, it says *WriteError, directory not found*. This happened because the user doesn't have a Windows PowerShell directory at C:\Users\gsingh\Documents location.

So, you need to create this directory manually; then, you should be able to run the preceding command successfully:

```
PS C:\Windows\system32> New-item -type file $profile


    Directory: C:\Users\gsingh\Documents\WindowsPowerShell


Mode                LastWriteTime     Length Name
----                -------------     ------ ----
-a---          1/6/2015   5:37 AM          0 Microsoft.PowerShell_profile.ps1
```

Now, let's configure the PoSH profile. Go to the PowerShell window and type notepad $profile. This will open a notepad where you can write your custom script. We will use it to import the XenDesktop module and Citrix snap-ins:

```
Asnp Citrix*
Import-module -name Citrix.XenDesktop.Admin
```

Now, you have configured your PoSH profile. You can test the path by running the following command:

```
Test-Path $profile
```

It should return the value `True`. You can always edit your PoSH profile by typing `notepad $profile` in the PowerShell prompt. Now, we will test our PoSH profile's functionality. To begin with, close the PowerShell window and reopen it to check that it's working fine.

 Make sure that you have set the **PowerShell execution policy** to **Remotely Signed** or **Unrestricted**.

Once you have launched the administrative shell, just type some basic commands to test the functionality:

```
Get-BrokerSite
```

The result is shown in the following screenshot:

```
Windows PowerShell
Windows PowerShell
Copyright (C) 2012 Microsoft Corporation. All rights reserved.

PS C:\Users\gsingh> Get-BrokerSite

BaseOU                               :
BrokerServiceGroupUid                : a9a16a66-a576-4eea-942d-0011a16daOc5
ColorDepth                           : TwentyFourBit
ConfigurationServiceGroupUid         : fafd48b7-3012-4bf4-9fee-51ddaf230193
DesktopGroupIconUid                  : 1
DnsResolutionEnabled                 : False
LicenseEdition                       : PLT
LicenseGraceSessionsRemaining        :
LicenseModel                         : Concurrent
LicenseServerName                    : XAO1.testlab.com
LicenseServerPort                    : 27000
LicensedSessionsActive               : 1
LicensingBurnInDate                  : 3/19/2014 12:00:00 AM
LicensingGraceHoursLeft              :
LicensingGracePeriodActive           : False
LicensingOutOfBoxGracePeriodActive   : False
MetadataMap                          : {}
Name                                 : AdminApps
SecureIcaRequired                    : False
TrustRequestsSentToTheXmlServicePort : False
```

 You can learn about the basic commands by issuing help commands:
```
Get-command -Module Citrix.Xendesktop.Admin
```

Checking controller services

Let's check the status of some of the XenDesktop controller services by their aliases through PowerShell. The following table lists FMA service PoSH aliases:

Service name	Alias
Broker Service	BROKER
Configuration Service	CONFIG
Host Service	HYP
Machine Creation Service	PROV
AD Identity Service	ACCT
Environment Test Service	ENVTEST
StoreFront Service	SF
Monitor Service	MONITOR
Configuration Logging Service	LOG
Delegated Administrative Service	ADMIN

The command used to check the status of the services is: Get<Alias>ServiceStatus. See the following screenshot for example commands:

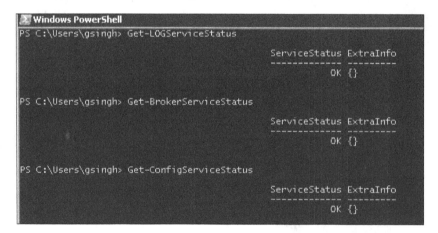

There are some important return codes other than OK for services status; type help Get-<Alias>Service Status -Full for more details.

You can write a simple PowerShell script to know the status of the controller service as shown here:

```
Code Begins -----------
"Checking Services Status............."
Write-Host "Broker Service" -Backgroundcolor "red" -foregroundcolor
"black"
Get-BrokerServiceStatus | Select service* | format-list
Write-Host "Log Service" -Backgroundcolor "Green" -foregroundcolor
"black"
Get-LogServiceStatus | Select service* |format-list
Write-Host "StoreFront Service" -Backgroundcolor "yellow"
-foregroundcolor "black"
Get-SFServiceStatus | Select service* |format-list
Code end .......................................
```

Checking the DB version

We can use PowerShell cmdlets to check a DB Schema's installed version and the available upgrade options, as shown in the following screenshot:

```
PS C:\scripts> Get-BrokerController

ActiveSiteServices                    : {ControllerReaper, ControllerNameCacheRefresh, Licensing, BrokerReaper...}
AssociatedHypervisorConnectionUids    : {3}
ControllerVersion                     : 7.5.0.4526
DNSName                               : XA01.testlab.com
DesktopsRegistered                    : 2
LastActivityTime                      : 1/6/2015 7:57:39 AM
LastStartTime                         : 1/6/2015 4:49:51 AM
MachineName                           : TESTLAB\XA01
MetadataMap                           : {}
OSType                                : Win32NT
OSVersion                             : 6.1.7601.65536
SID                                   : S-1-5-21-1496689503-1969313586-3789369547-1105
State                                 : Active
Uid                                   : 1


PS C:\scripts> Get-BrokerInstalledDbVersion

Major  Minor  Build  Revision
-----  -----  -----  --------
7      5      0      0
```

Checking the desktop machine details

You can check the desktop broker and machine details with the following commands:

- `Get-BrokerDesktop`
- `Get-BrokerMachine`

Refer to the following screenshot for visual examples:

```
PS C:\scripts> Get-BrokerDesktop | select DesktopGroupName

DesktopGroupName
----------------
Windows 7 VDI - Persistent
Windows 7 VDI - Persistent
Admins - Desktops


PS C:\scripts> Get-Brokermachine | select machinename

MachineName
-----------
TESTLAB\VDI-WIN7-01
TESTLAB\VDI-WIN7-02
TESTLAB\XA02
```

You can also filter desktop details with other relevant parameters such as `Desktopkind`, `UID`, and so on. Make sure you explore the options.

Managing identity pools

Identity pools are managed by the AD Identity service and we can check the status of identity pools and the provisioning scheme by using the following commands:

- `Get-AcctIdentityPool`
- `Get-ProvScheme`

Disconnect/logoff settings for desktops

The disconnect/logoff functionality has been removed with effect from the XenDesktop 4.0 release and it can be controlled only with the PoSH and XDSiteDiag tool now. Let's take a look at the available options:

- **View all disconnect options**: This is shown here:

```
PS C:\scripts> Get-BrokerDesktopGroup -PublishedName "Windows 7 VDI" | Select *PeakDisc*, *extend* | format-list

OffPeakDisconnectAction              : Nothing
OffPeakDisconnectTimeout             : 0
PeakDisconnectAction                 : Nothing
PeakDisconnectTimeout                : 0
OffPeakExtendedDisconnectAction      : Nothing
OffPeakExtendedDisconnectTimeout     : 0
PeakExtendedDisconnectAction         : Nothing
PeakExtendedDisconnectTimeout        : 0
```

- **Configuring extended disconnect settings with PoSH**: This is shown here:

```
PS C:\scripts> Set-BrokerDesktopGroup -Name "Win*" -PeakExtendedDisconnectAction suspend -PeakExtendedDisconnectTimeout
5
PS C:\scripts> Get-BrokerDesktopGroup -PublishedName "Windows 7 VDI" | Select *PeakDisc*, *extend* | format-list

OffPeakDisconnectAction          : Nothing
OffPeakDisconnectTimeout         : 0
PeakDisconnectAction             : Nothing
PeakDisconnectTimeout            : 0
OffPeakExtendedDisconnectAction  : Nothing
OffPeakExtendedDisconnectTimeout : 0
PeakExtendedDisconnectAction     : Suspend
PeakExtendedDisconnectTimeout    : 5
```

 Similarly, you can manage XenDesktop policies and other settings through PoSH. More cmdlets are available from Citrix to help you troubleshoot your XenDesktop environment; you can read more by visiting http://support.citrix.com/proddocs/topic/xenapp-xendesktop-75/cds-sdk-cmdlet-help.html.

Summary

We now have a fair idea of all the tools that can help us in troubleshooting a Citrix XenDesktop environment. Also, we have learned the importance of implementing these tools for different troubleshooting methodologies within the scope of XenDesktop environments.

In the next chapter, we will be using the knowledge gained in these chapters to troubleshoot issues based on different aspects, ranging from initial XenDesktop deployment to advanced configuration and integration with third-party tools.

3
Getting Around Installation Issues

In our last two chapters, we gained a basic knowledge of the Citrix XenDesktop architecture and the toolkit required to build a strong foundation for troubleshooting. We are now good to get started with troubleshooting different issues arising in the XenDesktop environment. We will start from the basics by troubleshooting the common issues that every administrator might face while installing and configuring Citrix XenDesktop for the first time.

In this chapter, we will cover the following topics:

* Dealing with prerequisite issues
* Overcoming database service account issues
* Taming licensing issues
* Getting around site creation issues

Prerequisites

The Citrix XenDesktop installer automatically deploys all prerequisites, such as the .NET Framework and, Visual Studio C++ components, if they don't exist on the system and are required for installation.

For hardware prerequisites, you need to ensure that you have at least a 3 GB RAM on the Controller server, if you are doing a proof-of-concept deployment on a single server that will be configured as Controller, Studio, Director, Storefront, and also for licensing. The actual hardware sizing of your environment will be done on the basis of this analysis and customer requirements. This is covered later in *Chapter 7, Troubleshooting Performance*.

To know more about all the system requirements to configure Citrix XenDesktop, you can refer to the Citrix eDocs at `http://docs.citrix.com/en-us/xenapp-and-xendesktop/7-6/xad-system-requirements-76.html`.

Another important aspect that we need take care of before starting our XenDesktop deployment is to make sure that we allow the relevant firewall exceptions to allow a smooth deployment of XenDesktop.

Refer to the following communication ports table that every Citrix administrator should know before starting the deployment:

Source	Destination	Ports
XenDesktop Delivery Controller	Citrix License Server	TCP 27000, TCP 7279
	VMWare vCenter Server	TCP 80, 443
	SQL Database Server	TCP 1433, 1434
	Active Directory	UDP 636, 389
	VDI Subnet	TCP 80, TCP 135, TCP 3389
	Citrix Storefront Server	TCP 80, 443
ICA clients/Receiver LAN	XenDesktop Delivery Controller	TCP 1494, 2598
Citrix Storefront	XenDesktop Delivery Controller	TCP 80, 443
Citrix NetScaler	XenDesktop Delivery Controller	TCP 8080/80, TCP 443, TCP 1494, TCP 2598
VDI Subnet	XenDesktop Delivery Controller	TCP 80, TCP 8080, TCP 3268

Dealing with prerequisite issues

With the XenDesktop 7.x release, the prerequisites are automatically installed and there have hardly been any issues reported regarding the installation of prerequisites for XenDesktop components.

The only issue that has been faced by many admins is that you might see the following screen after launching Studio:

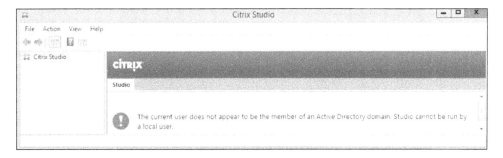

This happens when you install XenDesktop and its components with a local admin account. So, always make sure that you install a XenDesktop product suite with a domain account that has administrative privileges. Otherwise, you might end up with this confusing error. Apart from this, there have been no major issues reported regarding the prerequisites so far.

To resolve the preceding error, you need to uninstall Citrix XenDesktop and reinstall it using a domain account with administrative privileges on the Windows server where you will install the XenDesktop product components.

 XenDesktop requires a SQL database and the account used to install XenDesktop must have the required DB permissions on the database server; otherwise, you may face issues with XenDesktop site creation.

Overcoming database service account issues

While installing XenDesktop, you need to make sure that the service account or admin account that you will use to configure and build the XenDesktop site has the appropriate rights to the database server.

We have seen issues where site creation has failed if the appropriate DB rights are not given to the account being used to configure the site. Let's take a look at the following DB rights required to configure the XenDesktop site:

DB operation	Function	Server roles	Database permission
Database creation	Creates an empty database for use by the XenDesktop site.	`dbcreator`	
Schema creation	Creates all service-specific database schemas and adds the first controller to the site.	`securityadmin`	`db_owner`
Add controller	Adds the controller (other than the first) to the site.	`securityadmin`	`db_owner`
Add controller (mirror server)	Adds the controller login to the database server currently in the mirror role of a mirrored XenDesktop database.	`securityadmin`	
Remove controller	Removes the controller from the site.		`db_owner`
Schema update	Applies schema updates/hotfixes.		`db_owner`

 The database permissions table has been taken from a Citrix Knowledge Center article. For more details, refer to the article at `http://support.citrix.com/article/CTX127998`.

Taming licensing issues

If you have been working with the Citrix XenApp suite for a long time, you might be well aware of the licensing issues and their impact. Licensing issues are most commonly seen with mismatched cases of the product version and license server configuration on the farm and site level.

While installing XenDesktop, always make sure that you are pointing your XenDesktop site to the correct license server. If you have configured your Controller server version as XenDesktop Platinum and your license server has Enterprise licenses, it will show license errors to the users, as shown in the following screenshot:

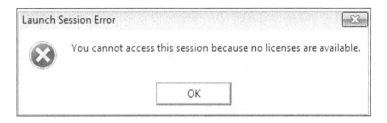

 Also, make sure that your license server is upgraded to the latest version, as XenDesktop 7.6 doesn't support the license server version prior to 11.12.1. Citrix also recommends to install the latest license server before deploying XenDesktop and this will be first thing that Citrix Support will ask you before looking into any licensing issues.

You will see **Event 1152** in the event log viewer for Citrix Broker Service, as shown in the following screenshot:

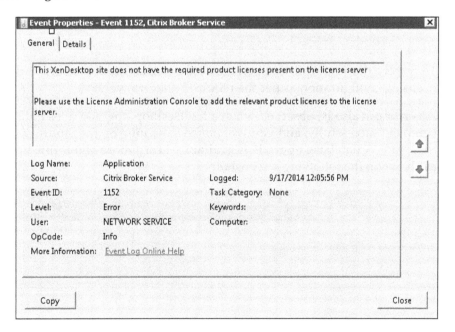

There are multiple reasons for this particular error. The following are the two most commonly listed reasons for this error:

- The error can be encountered if Studio is configured for an incorrect licensing server, license version, platform, and so on. Open the Studio console to verify the details:

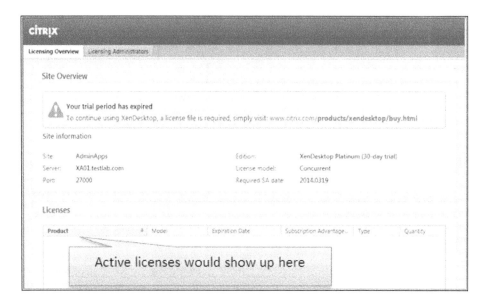

To resolve this issue, please open the Citrix Studio console to correct the licensing configuration as per the required platform version.

- An error can also be observed when a XenDesktop upgrade does not complete successfully, and you will notice a warning on the Studio console that reads **A database upgrade is available. Learn more about this upgrade**, as shown in the following screenshot:

Sometimes, when there is a firewall blocking the license server ports, a XenDesktop site upgrade doesn't complete successfully and results in this error. For details on the licensing ports, let's take a look at the ports table, which we have already explained in this chapter in the *Prerequisites* section.

To resolve this issue, proceed with the database upgrade from Citrix Studio.

 You can download the Citrix Licensing troubleshooting guide from `http://support.citrix.com/servlet/KbServlet/download/11186-102-665786/Troubleshooting.pdf` for a basic understanding of licensing and some common issues.

Site creation issues

There are some issues reported that might arise while creating XenDesktop sites due to the following reasons:

- Insufficient database permissions
- Insufficient hypervisor connection permissions
- Domain permissions
- Incorrect configuration for storage pool

Insufficient database permissions

As highlighted in the *Overcoming database service account issues* section, it is very important to make sure that the service account you are using for the DB connection to create the XenDesktop site has sufficient permissions. Otherwise, the site creation may fail due to insufficient permission errors. You can refer to the DB permissions table given in the *Overcoming database service account issues* section.

Hypervisor connection permissions

Similar to the DB permissions, you also need to make sure that the admin account being used to create and administer a XenDesktop site has proper permissions for the hypervisor cluster. Otherwise, you might not be able to create the XenDesktop Machine Catalog and might see some weird errors on the Studio console.

For detailed permissions of each type of hypervisor, please refer to the articles at:

- `http://docs.citrix.com/en-us/xenapp-and-xendesktop/7-6/xad-build-new-enviroment/xad-install-prep-host-vmware.html`
- `http://docs.citrix.com/en-us/xenapp-and-xendesktop/7-6/xad-build-new-enviroment/xad-install-prep-host-msscvmm.html`

For XenDesktop Controller to communicate successfully with XenServer, you need permissions assigned to the Active Directory account in XenServer. The minimum permissions for an AD account to communicate with XenServer don't seem to be documented anywhere but, from testing, it looks like the VM admin role has the minimum requirements.

Domain permissions

Domain permissions are very essential for XenDesktop site creation; you cannot use a local admin account to administer a XenDesktop site joined to a corporate domain. You should use a domain account having administrative rights to the controller server for administering your XD sites. Otherwise, you might see an insufficient rights error while opening the Studio console.

Incorrect configuration for storage pools

You also need to make sure that your storage data stores are configured correctly with your hypervisor hosts. Incorrect storage connections can cause your MCS- or PVS-based machine creation wizard to fail.

Refer to the following screenshot for an MCS catalog failure due to incorrect storage configuration:

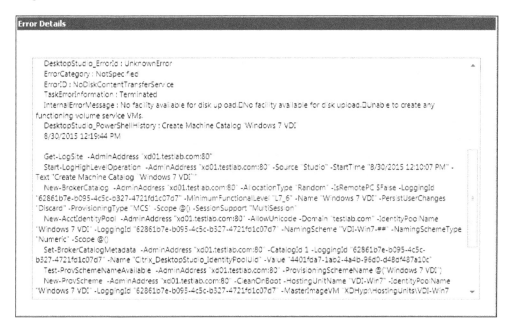

The preceding error is reported if you are using an SSD drive while creating an AMI master image for your MCS deployment on the Amazon EC2 cloud. Amazon and Citrix are aware of the issue but they haven't released a fix as of now.

There is a known issue with the AWS plugin for **Elastic Network Interface** (**ENI**) that gets created during the image copy process of the MCS deployment wizard on the AWS EC2 cloud. AWS deletes this ENI interface automatically after the image copy process is completed; at the same time, XenDesktop also tries to delete it, which causes duplicate deletes and throws ENI a "Not Found Error".

AWS has provided a workaround for this issue by using magnetic or standard drives instead of SSD drives while preparing your master image, as shown in the following screenshot:

For a detailed step-by-step guide on how to deploy VDIs using MCS on the AWS EC2 cloud, please refer to the Citrix deployment guide at http://docs.citrix.com/content/dam/docs/en-us/ xenapp-xendesktop/xenapp-xendesktop-7-6/downloads/ Deploy_XenApp_and_XenDesktop_7_5_with_Amazon_VPC.pdf.

You might face similar or other issues with your storage configuration while using different hypervisors. To resolve such issues, it is always recommended to follow the Citrix deployment guides available for particular vendors.

Summary

We should now have a good understanding of prerequisite requirements, common issues related to licensing, database permissions, site creation, and many more topics that can help us in deploying a Citrix XenDesktop site successfully and troubleshooting some of the common issues that might arise while installing and configuring the XenDesktop site for the first time.

In our next chapter, we will focus on the VDA registration issues that might arise while configuring a MCS- and PVS-based Machine Catalog.

4
Overcoming VDA Registration Problems

In our last chapter, we discussed the common problems related to XenDesktop deployment and installation that may arise while installing and configuring it for the first time. We will now be dealing with the most common and important VDA registration problems that we often face while working with the XenDesktop product suite. Every Citrix administrator who has worked on the XenDesktop platform may have faced VDA registration problems. Sometimes, these issues make a Citrix admin's life a nightmare, if not tackled with proper troubleshooting skills.

This chapter is focused on acquiring skills related to the VDA registration process and troubleshooting different kinds of VDA registration problems that you may encounter in a XenDesktop environment. The skills acquired in this chapter will allow you to handle any kind of VDA registration issue without any major headache and also make your life easy.

In this chapter, we will cover the following points:

- Getting familiar with the VDA registration process
- Starting with the basics – the event viewer
- Configuring the firewall
- Troubleshooting DNS resolution issues
- Overcoming NTP or time synchronization issues
- Conquering domain membership problems
- Working with multiple network adapters
- Working with **service principal name** (**SPN**)

- Surpassing DDC FQDN issues
- Getting familiar with local group policies and VDA communication
- Solving the .NET framework exceptions
- A basic troubleshooting flowchart
- Troubleshooting using the VDA and Broker Service logs and other tools

Getting familiar with the VDA registration process

The VDA registration process involves two major components: **Virtual Desktop Agent (VDA)** and **Desktop Delivery Controller (DDC)**. These two components interact with each other for a successful VDA registration.

VDA is a collection of drivers and services that are loaded on to the desktop or host machine where you want to establish a connection. The VDA agent contacts one of the Delivery Controllers as per the configured DDC server-list and registers itself to be available to users, based upon the desktop groups/catalogs configured in the SQL data store. The list of DDC servers can be configured in the following ways:

- While installing the VDA agent on host machines
- Using Windows registry discovery
- Through Active Directory GPO
- Through Citrix policies

DDC is a component that enables you to deliver virtual desktops to endusers. It allows you to effectively manage, maintain, and provision all virtual desktop connections with a single management console called Studio. The Delivery Controller also manages the licensing and data store that contains the static configuration information for the XenDesktop site.

 To test the VDA registration process, you can simply restart **Citrix Desktop Service** on the host machine and verify whether it registers itself with the Controller or not.

I have included a small flow diagram to show how the VDA registration takes place. The following diagram is self-explanatory and the details mentioned around each step make it easier for readers to understand:

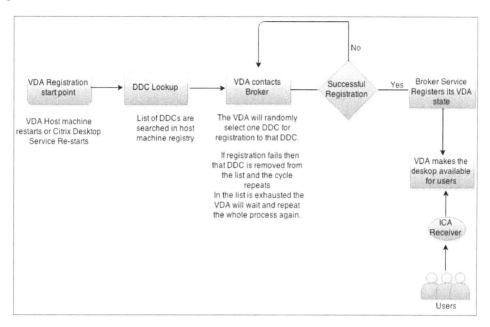

Starting with the basics – the event viewer

One of the most common errors that you may encounter in a XenDesktop deployment is your VDA getting stuck in the unregistered state. Until the VDA is registered with the Controller, you won't be able to deliver virtual desktops to end users.

Troubleshooting any issue in a Windows environment starts with the event viewer. This is the starting point for any administrator looking to resolve a problem affecting their Windows server environment. The same applies when troubleshooting XenDesktop VDA registration issues.

So, whenever you see the VDA state as unregistered on the Studio console, open up the Windows event viewer on the host machine where VDA is installed and check the application logs. You will notice an error similar to the following screenshot:

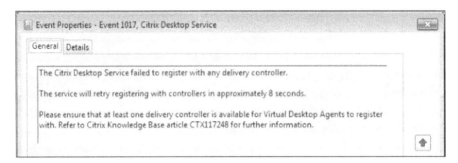

The VDA or Broker Service has failed to register itself with the available controller servers. This means that either the registry entry for the list of DDC servers doesn't have any valid entries or there are some other communication issues.

There are some famous event IDs that every Citrix admin should be aware of while troubleshooting VDA registration issues. This is the sequence of events that you will see on the VDA host machine experiencing communication issues:

Event ID	Description	Explanation
Warning Event ID 1014	The Citrix Desktop Service has lost contact with the Citrix Desktop Delivery Controller Service on server ddc01.testlab.com. The service will now attempt to register again.	This happens when no DDC server is listening at the Controller address or there is an issue with the SOAP service.
Warning Event ID 1002	The Citrix Desktop Service cannot connect to the Delivery Controller at http://ddc01.testlab.com:80/Citrix/CdsController/Registrar (IP address 10.33.1.21)	This happens when there is a time sync issue between the VDA machine and the Delivery Controller.
Warning Event ID 1017	The Citrix Desktop Service failed to register with any Delivery Controller. The service will retry registering with Controller in approximately 17 seconds.	Check for Delivery Controllers, there should be at least one Delivery Controller online to serve the VDA agent registrations.

Event ID	Description	Explanation
Warning Event ID 1022	The Citrix Desktop Service failed to register with any Controllers in the last 2 minutes. The service will now try to register with Controllers at a reduced rate of every 2 minutes.	Check for domain controller ports if these are allowed from VDA. This error may occur when the VDA is not able to access a DC on port `3268` (Microsoft Global Catalog). The VDA must communicate with the DC during the registration process in order to validate its list of configured Controllers.
Warning Event ID 1012	The Citrix Desktop Service successfully registered with Delivery Controller `ddc01. testlab.com` (IP Address `10.33.1.21`).	This is a successful registration event.
Warning Event ID 1048	The Citrix Desktop Service is re-registering with the DDC: `NotificationManager:` `NotificationServiceThread:` `WCF failure or rejection by broker (DDC: ddc01. testlab.com)`	This happens when there are name lookup issues on the VDA machines or DNS lookup failures. Check if your DNS is working correctly and whether you are able to resolve the FQDN of DDC servers. You can try troubleshooting by making hostfile entries and removing them for NetBIOS to FQDN resolution.
Information Event ID 0	The error that occurs is *The description for event ID 0 from source Self-service Plug-in cannot be found. Either the component that raises this event is not installed on your local computer or the installation is corrupted. You can install or repair the component on the local computer.*	This is a follow-up event to Event 1048.
Warning Event ID 1001	The Citrix Desktop Service failed to obtain a list of Delivery Controllers with which to register.	Make sure that the VDA machine is able to contact the domain controller and is a part of the correct Active Directory domain.

Firewall configuration

If you have a firewall between your VDA and DDC subnets, make sure that it is properly configured to allow successful Controller communication. If you find that the firewall is interfering with the VDA registration process, you can try disabling it to successfully test and verify the VDA registration.

By default, the FMA architecture in XenDesktop 7.x uses TCP port 80 for communication. So, while planning to configure firewalls, we should be aware of all the ports that our VDA is using. If required, this port can be changed using the BrokerService.exe command. So, to make sure that you are correctly configuring the right exclusions in the firewall, it is always beneficial to check the port by using the BrokerService.exe command, as shown in the following screenshot:

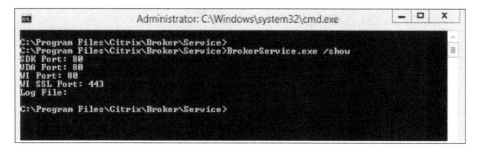

Troubleshooting DNS resolution issues

DNS resolution is one of the most common issues that we see while troubleshooting VDA registration issues. Whenever you see an unregistered state on the Studio console for VDA host machines and you are sure that the list of DDC servers is configured correctly, you should start troubleshooting for network and DNS resolution.

Try starting with the ping command that needs to be run from the VDA and DDC servers respectively. You should be able to ping and resolve the FQDN name for the DDC servers from the VDA host machine and vice versa.

Scenario – VDA is not able to reach the Delivery Controller

You start with the `ping` command and find that you are not able to ping the Delivery Controller from the VDA machine, as shown in the following screenshot:

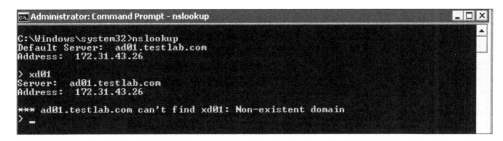

The next step we need to perform is to verify its entry in the DNS, so we need to run the `nslookup` command, as shown here:

Citrix Studio shows the machine as unregistered:

We found that the system administrator has accidentally deleted the DNS host record for the Delivery Controller server due to which no machine was able to register with the Delivery Controller. I replicated this issue in my lab by deleting the DNS entry and re-creating it to resolve the issue.

After the re-creation of the DNS entry for the Delivery Controller, the VDA machine was successfully registered with the Delivery Controller, as shown in the following screenshot:

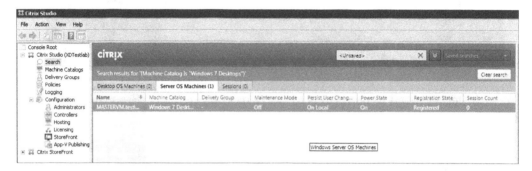

Similarly, you can encounter different issues with the DNS lookup in your environment and you can start with the basics, using the `ping` and `nslookup` commands to troubleshoot. For detailed troubleshooting, you can use the **XDPing** tool, as explained in *Chapter 2, Troubleshooting Toolkit for Citrix XenDesktop®*, to look at the DNS resolution issues.

Make sure that you have reverse DNS lookup enabled along with forward lookup in your DNS setup. This is essential for proper VDA registration.

We have seen DNS resolution issues with Infoblox appliances; the devices are not fast enough for the DNS resolution that is expected for VDA registration. We are not sure if this has been resolved in their latest release. The workaround for this issue is to test it by adding a host entry on the VDA host machine with the FQDN names of the Controller servers that will resolve any VDA registration issue due to these devices.

Overcoming time synchronization issues

Time synchronization is done by Kerberos and is very important, as Kerberos allows a time skew of less than 5 minutes for the time difference between client and server. If the time difference between the VDA and Controllers is too big (more than 5 minutes), there is a fair chance that the tickets will get timed out, causing communication to fail.

To troubleshoot this issue, you can make use of the **W32tm** utility or PowerShell. The following screenshot shows how to find the time difference between your controller and VDA machine by issuing a simple `w32tm` query:

Always make sure that the system time on all the systems is within a small margin and doesn't vary with a big difference considering the Kerberos skew.

Conquering domain membership problems

Being a Windows or Citrix administrator, you may have experienced issues with machine domain memberships. The machine will appear to be working fine, but will sometimes give weird errors related to domain membership.

These issues tend to cause problems with the VDA registrations as well. So, it is always recommended that if you see any similar issues in your environment, try to remove the machine from the domain and then re-join it to the domain. After restart, the VDA machine should successfully register the VDA with the controllers.

For domain membership problems, you can enable Broker Agent logging, which can give you an insight into what is going wrong when the VDA is failing to register with the Controller server.

The example error log will look like this:

```
BrokerAgent:ConstructAndResolveRegistrarNames: Using IP Addresses; IP
172.31.38.21, Hostname xd01.testlab.com, m_UseIpv6Registration = False
BrokerAgent:=========>>>>> Attempting registration with following
controller(s): xd01.testlab.com(172.31.38.21)
BrokerAgent:AttemptRegistrationWithSingleDdc: Attempting to talk to
controller...
BrokerAgent:AgentHeartBeat m_connectionId = S-1-5-21-3723409013-
3417450140-2352212834-1105
BrokerAgent:CurrentSettingsVersion is 0;
BrokerAgent: We are attempting to register with DDC 'xd01.testlab.
com'; Previous successful registration was with DDC ''
BrokerAgent:Sending CurrentSettingsVersion = 0 to DDC to force policy
delivery
BrokerAgent:Registration request 7.6.0.5026 Windows 2008 R2 Service
Pack 1 Microsoft Windows NT 6.1.7601 Service Pack1. S-1-5-21-
3723409013-3417450140-2352212834
BrokerAgent:request.WorkerCapabilities CBP1_5
BrokerAgent:request.WorkerCapabilities MultiSession
BrokerAgent:Registration multi-session Type MultiSession.
BrokerAgent:AttemptRegistrationWithSingleDdc: Failed to register with
http://Xd01.testlab.com:80/Citrix/CdsController/IRegistrar. WCF Fault
with detail CallbackCommunicationError, message 'Fail worker callback
using SPN HOST/MasterVM and IP address 172.31.21.13'
BrokerAgent: TimedEventLogWorkItemManager:
:ProcessWorkItemThreadBody - Processing
BrokerAgent:TimedEventLogWorkItemManager:
:ProcessWorkItemThreadBody - Sleeping 599999ms
BrokerAgent: Attempt Registration: Could not register with any
controllers. Waiting to try again in 120000 ms. Multi-forest - False
```

The preceding error indicates that there is an issue with the registration of the VDA while talking to the Delivery Controller with the SPN name `MasterVM`. We should look at the VDA machine for any Winlogon event or related error that is restricting the VDA machine while talking to the Domain Controller making the registration fail.

In this case, we couldn't find any specific events. However, with the previous log we found that the SPN seems to be missing an FQDN entry for the VDA machine. The issue was resolved by entering the correct FQDN entry.

 We will see how to edit SPN entries for AD objects to resolve similar issues in the upcoming sections.

Multiple network adapters

There are reports that if you have multiple network adapters configured on the VDA machines, it may interfere with the secure communication between the VDA and controller servers, causing the registration to fail.

It's recommended to have only a single network adapter configured on all the VDA machines that require registration with the Controller servers.

To troubleshoot issues where multiple network adapters are configured on the VDA host machines, it is recommended to disable the additional adapter and run the VDA registration test.

Service principal name

Microsoft **Windows Communication Foundation (WCF)** is used for the secure communication that happens between the VDA and DDC controller servers.

WCF communication uses the computer identity for endpoints participating in the communication and presents a **service principal name (SPN)** with the respective computer accounts. The SPN is normally a FQDN of the host machine.

The Controller server determines the SPN for virtual desktops using the servicePrincipalName attribute of the associated computer account in Active Directory. We can inspect the virtual desktop's computer account using tools, such as Active Directory Explorer, PowerShell commands using the Active Directory module, and so on.

If you don't see any entry in the servicePrincipalName attribute for the FQDN of the VDA host machine, try editing it manually to add the required FQDN entry. This should fix the VDA registration problems.

You can view and edit the SPN attribute by using Active Directory Administrative Center, as described in the following steps:

1. Log in to any domain controller or management server that has AD administrative tools installed.

2. Launch the **Active Directory Administrative Center** window, as shown in the following screenshot:

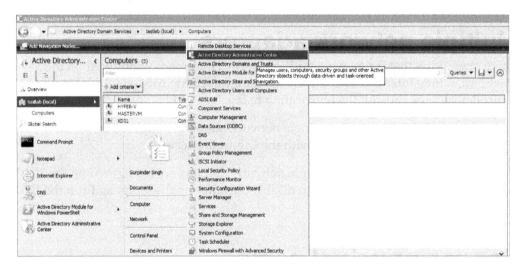

3. Expand your Active Directory site to select the VDA machine.

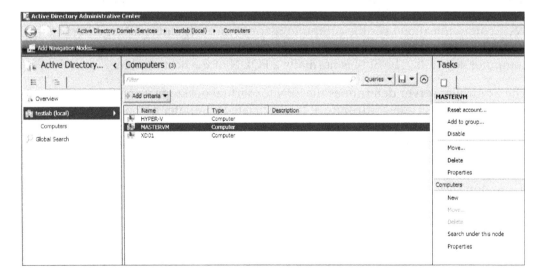

4. Now, click on **Extensions** to edit the attributes for the computer object.

5. Go to the **Attributes** tab and select the SPN to edit the entry.

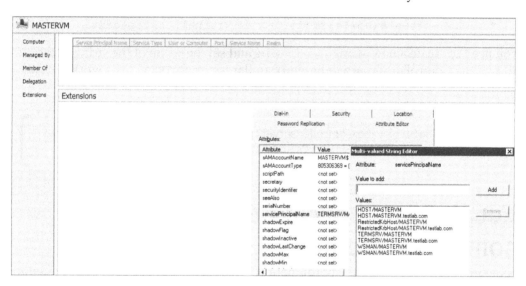

The highlighted SPN entries are required for successful VDA registration and if this is missing, you can edit it using Active Directory Administrative Center and fix the VDA registration issue for a particular VDA machine.

Surpassing DDC FQDN issues

We have also seen issues with the latest XenDesktop 7.x version where, sometimes, ListOfDDCs containing the FQDN of the DDC servers are not enough for successful VDA registrations.

In older versions, we used to configure a DNS alias for multiple Controllers to provide a DNS round robin load distribution among multiple servers. This doesn't work anymore with XenDesktop 7.x versions. So, it is recommended to use FQDN for all the Controller servers listed in the ListOfDDCs.

Sometimes, you have multiple Active Directory domains connected by an external trust and you want those VDAs from multiple domains to register to the Controller servers. In this scenario, it is necessary to create a registry key under the following relevant paths:

- HKLM\Software\Citrix\VirtualDesktopAgent\
- HKLM\Software\Wow6432Node\Citrix\VirtualDesktopAgent\

You need to create a new string ListOfSIDs and set the value of the string to the SIDs of the Controllers (space delimited) similar to ListOfDDCs, as a workaround for this issue.

 The SID for the Controller server can be found by initiating a PowerShell command Get-BrokerController on the Controller server.

Local group policies and VDA communication

Sometimes, in a more secure environment where local group policies are enforced to disallow network access, the VDA registration can fail.

Event ID 1208 and Event ID 1123 would be seen on the application logs of the virtual desktop. The event detail gives the following errors:

- *Ping request was rejected by the Citrix Desktop Delivery Controller Service. It may be unable to contact this machine. Check that there is not a firewall blocking connection.*
- *Failed to apply settings on the Virtual Desktop Agent on machine <SID – Reference Number>. Reason: The caller was not authenticated by the service.*

To resolve this issue, we need to grant a logon right on the **Access this computer from the network to the Controllers Security Group** setting. The Controller security group is created when the first Delivery Controller is installed and added to the Active Directory organizational unit.

You can also grant logon rights by completing one of the following tasks:

- Apply a group policy from the domain controller either to the domain as a whole or to an organizational unit containing the virtual desktops for the XenDesktop farm.

- Grant the rights by using a local policy on the virtual desktops. It might be necessary to restart the virtual desktops after setting this policy, to force the policy to update and register with the Desktop Delivery Controller.

 For more details on this issue and its resolutions, please refer to the Citrix Knowledge Center article at `http://support.citrix.com/article/CTX117449`.

Solving .NET framework exceptions

As we are aware, XenDesktop brokering works on WCF. This is a part of the Microsoft .NET framework where the communication works on channels and activities for the VDA communication and these activities have the following timeouts defined:

- **Open timeout**: Timeout defined for the amount of time it can wait once the connection is opened

- **Close timeout**: Timeout defined for the duration of time to dispose the client proxy

- **Send timeout**: Timeout defined to send a message to a client

- **Receive timeout**: Timeout defined to receive a response from a client once the message has been sent

Sometimes, due to these timeout settings, the VDA registration can fail and you will see the following exceptions reported on your screen: *Unhandled Exception: System. TimeoutException: The open operation did not complete within the allotted timeout of 00:00:05. The time allotted to this operation may have been a portion of a longer timeout.*

You will see this exception when the server registration takes more than 5 seconds to complete. You should look in the network trace to find out what is going on with the network that is causing this delay and hence the timeout errors. You can increase the timeout value to resolve these timeouts as a workaround, but you should always analyze the network trace to find the root cause of the delay to configure it accordingly.

A basic troubleshooting flowchart

In a nutshell, every admin must follow this flowchart given by Citrix to troubleshoot all VDA registration issues:

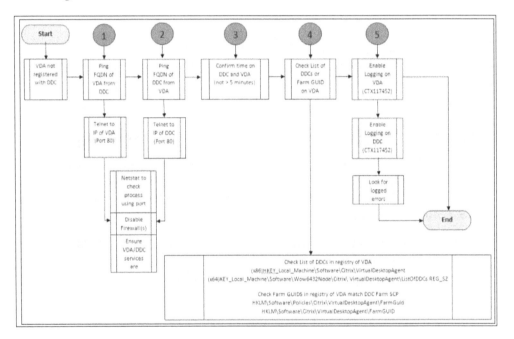

 For more details on the flowchart, please visit the Citrix article at http://support.citrix.com/article/CTX136668.

For basic troubleshooting, you can use the XDPing utility from Citrix that provides very good basic diagnostic information about troubleshooting VDA registration issues. The download link details can be found in *Chapter 2, Troubleshooting Toolkit for Citrix XenDesktop®*.

Troubleshooting using the VDA and Broker Service logs and other tools

There can be some scenarios where basic troubleshooting won't be of much help and you need to dig down more into the brokering traces for expert level troubleshooting. You need to enable logging for both VDA and Broker Services and it requires a tool that can parse the traces for better analysis.

 Microsoft Service Trace Viewer is a very good tool to pass and read trace files. The tool is a part of the Windows SDK that can be downloaded from http://www.microsoft.com/en-au/download/details.aspx?id=11310.

Once the Windows SDK is installed, you can locate the tool at `<Installation_Drive>\Program Files\Microsoft SDKs\Windows\v6.0\Bin Tools\SvcTraceViewer.exe`.

You can refer to *Chapter 2*, *Troubleshooting Toolkit for Citrix XenDesktop®*, for details on how to enable VDA and Broker Service logs.

The Broker Service thread will provide you with the information on multiple threads and it can be confusing and time consuming to fetch the required details for effective troubleshooting. You can filter the desired logs that took more than 1 second to process, to get better results.

VDA communication is based on WCF and it is a subset of the Microsoft .NET framework. If you want to dig deep into troubleshooting VDA communication-related issues, you can use the Microsoft Service Trace Viewer tool (SvcTraceViewer). It has got a very nice GUI interface that is quite easy to understand and is used to troubleshoot .NET framework-related application issues.

Once you have this tool ready with you, the next step is to enable the VDA and Broker Service logging by editing the **config** files for both the services, as shown here:

```
<system.diagnostics>
    <sources>
        <source name="System.ServiceModel"
                switchValue="Information, ActivityTracing"
                propagateActivity="true">
        <listeners>
```

```
        <add name="traceListener"
            type="System.Diagnostics.XmlWriterTraceListener"
            initializeData= "D:\XDlogs\Traces.svclog" />
    </listeners>
  </source>
 </sources>
</system.diagnostics>
```

By enabling the traces, you will see that `Traces.svclog` is created in the subfolder `D:\XDLogs`. You can change the location as you wish.

Once we are ready with the log files, open Microsoft Trace Viewer by browsing to `C:\Program Files\Microsoft SDKs\Windows\v7.1\Bin` and selecting the `svctraceviewer.exe` file, as shown here:

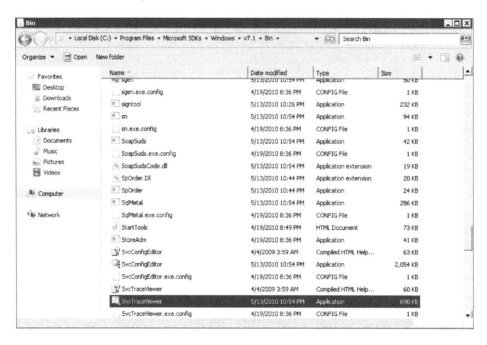

Once you open the trace to parse in Microsoft Trace Viewer and open the `svctrace`
file for Broker Service, you will see a screen similar to the following screenshot:

WCF trace activities are listed by creation time on the left-hand side pane and their
nested activities on the upper-right pane. All the errors are highlighted in red, which
can be easily spotted. In this example, the issue is caused by a timeout:

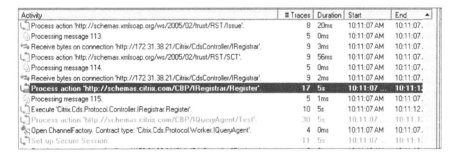

In order to read the error, you need to click on the **Set up Secure Session** link and press the *F4* key to display the detailed graphical-view stats, as shown here:

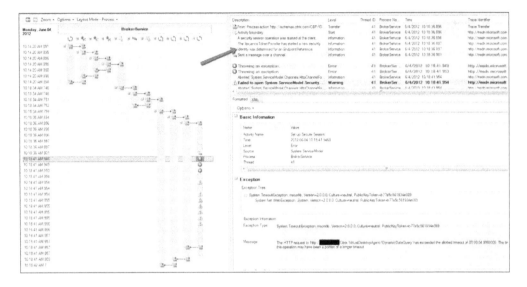

You need to select the first error (the red cross) on the left pane, to see the detailed statistics on the right pane. Make a note of the **Identity was determined for an Endpoint Reference** message, it's very important for registration. It will give you the details of the related SPN of the device that is throwing the error.

A more detailed analysis can be done using Wireshark but that requires more effort and sufficiently good skills to use the tool and decode the trace.

You can learn more about tracing and troubleshooting a WCF trace by visiting the MSDN hyperlink at `https://msdn.microsoft.com/en-us/library/aa751795(v=vs.110).aspx`.

Summary

By now we have a good understanding of the basic and advance level troubleshooting skills that are required to troubleshoot any kind of VDA registration issue that occurs in your XenDesktop environment.

In our next chapter, we will focus on the Citrix end users session launch-related issues that may arise while users are working locally or remotely and launching their virtual desktops for their daily tasks.

5
Conquering Citrix Session Launch Difficulties

In the last chapter, we discussed the VDA registration process and the related problems and issues that every Citrix administrator must know about while managing a XenDesktop infrastructure. We will now move forward to issues that are most commonly reported by endusers: Citrix launch issues. Every Citrix administrator who has worked on the XenDesktop platform should be very well versed with the Citrix VDA launch process.

This chapter focuses on gaining skills about the VDA launch process and its related problem areas that can help Citrix administrators to troubleshoot different kinds of VDA launch problems encountered in a XenDesktop environment.

In this chapter, we will cover the following points:

- Getting familiar with the VDA launch process
- Basic troubleshooting with Citrix Director
- Common Citrix XenDesktop launch issues
- Overcoming Citrix WI or StoreFront port mapping issues
- Configuring and analyzing logs

Getting familiar with the VDA launch process

The VDA launch process involves enumerating, brokering, and connecting to XenDesktop resources. There are multiple communication checkpoints in this process and it can be a challenging task, for someone who isn't familiar with the product, to troubleshoot or pinpoint problem areas.

In order to understand logon issues better, we should first understand the logon processes shown in the following diagram. The following diagram illustrates the logon process that is focused on internal users. There are some additional steps that are required for external remote access via NetScaler Gateway.

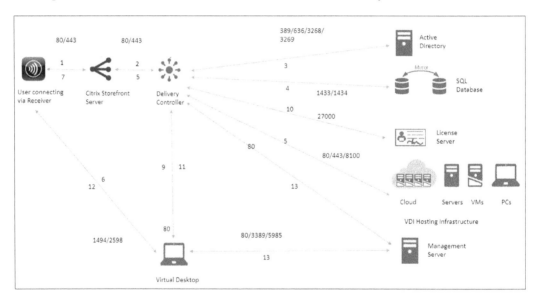

We have listed the steps that explain the VDA logon process and the flow of communication as follows:

1. The user enters credentials to the StoreFront web URL to log in.

2. StoreFront passes the credentials to Active Directory, which then does the validation check and passes it over to the Delivery Controller to enumerate applications.

3. The Controller queries the Microsoft Active Directory with the supplied user's credentials for a successful user authorization.

4. The Controller performs another query on the site database for the enduser's assigned delivery groups on ports `1434` and `1433` for assigned application/ desktop enumeration.

5. Now, the published applications and desktops are presented to the user on the StoreFront interface. The user clicks on one of the published/assigned desktop delivery groups to start a XenDesktop session. Now, the controller performs a query to the hypervisor about the status of the desktops for that particular delivery group.

6. The Controller validates the identification to StoreFront for the assigned desktop dedicated to this particular session.

7. StoreFront generates an ICA file and passes it to the Citrix Receiver for the required virtual desktop that is identified by the hypervisor.

8. Citrix Receiver connects to the specific virtual desktop through the ICA connection that the controller has allocated for this session.

9. License verification happens from the VDA to the controller for a valid license file.

10. The Controller then queries the Citrix License server to verify ticket validation for the enduser.

11. Session policies are passed to the VDA through the Controller, which then get applied to the virtual desktop.

12. Citrix Receiver completes the launch process and then displays the virtual desktop to the enduser.

For administration purposes, you can use Desktop Director and Desktop Studio tools installed on the management server to manage the desktops.

The NetScaler authentication steps are as follows:

1. Users browse a public URL on a HTTPS secure SSL connection.

2. Authentication takes place on NetScaler for Active Directory, Radius, or SAML if configured.

3. NetScaler forwards the user AD credentials to the StoreFront server over a virtual IP configured for load balancing the StoreFront service on NetScaler.

4. After retrieving the AD credentials from NetScaler, StoreFront passes them to the Active Directory Domain Controller, which completes the validation check and passes the credentials to the Delivery Controller. Then, the steps follow as explained in the preceding steps from step 3 of the VDA launch process.

We explained Citrix StoreFront and NetScaler integration in *Chapter 11, Troubleshooting NetScaler® Integration Issues*. To learn about integration in detail, you can refer to this chapter.

Basic troubleshooting with Citrix Director

The two basic tools provided with Citrix XenDesktop for helpdesk and administrators assist us in investigating issues within our environment; they are Citrix Studio and Citrix Director.

The Director has two views depending upon permissions: a helpdesk view and an administrator view. The following are the permissions that are available to control the level of access your helpdesk team and XenDesktop administrators have:

Administrator role	Permissions in Director
Full administrator	Complete access to all views and can perform all commands, including shadowing a user's session, enabling maintenance mode, and exporting trend data.
Delivery group administrator	Complete access to all views and can perform all commands, including shadowing a user's session, enabling maintenance mode, and exporting trends data. Can access all views and see all objects in specified scopes as well as global information.
Read-only administrator	Can download reports from HDX channels and can export trend data using the **Export** option in the **Trends** view. Cannot perform any other command or change anything in the views.
HelpDesk administrator	Can access only the **HelpDesk** and **User Detail** views and can view only the objects that the administrator is delegated to manage; can shadow a user's session and perform commands for that user. Performs maintenance mode operations and uses power control options for desktop OS machines. Cannot access the **Dashboard**, **Trends**, or **Filters** views and also cannot use the power control options for server OS machines.
Machine catalog administrator	No access. This administrator is not supported for Director and cannot view data.
Host administrator	No access. This administrator is not supported for Director and cannot view data.

For more details on permissions, please refer to `http://docs.citrix.com/en-us/xenapp-and-xendesktop/7-6.html`.

The most important view that you will see here is the administrative view. It offers additional features compared to others and allows you to have historical views with data stored that can be viewed anytime for a single hour, days, months, and years.

On the dashboard, you can always see the average time taken for user logon, active sessions, failed machines, connections, and so on. This is shown in the following screenshot:

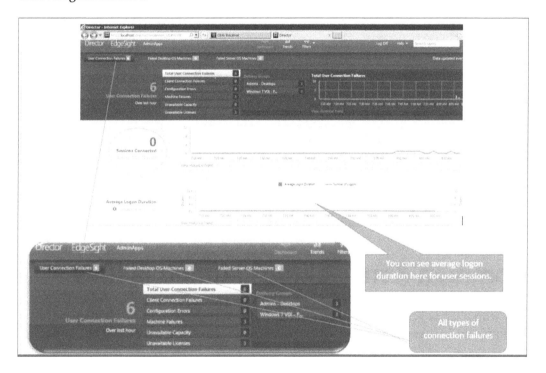

You can also view more granular details from the details option for users, such as currently loaded processes, HDX performance, launched applications, name of the VDA, memory/CPU usage statistics, policies applied, and so on:

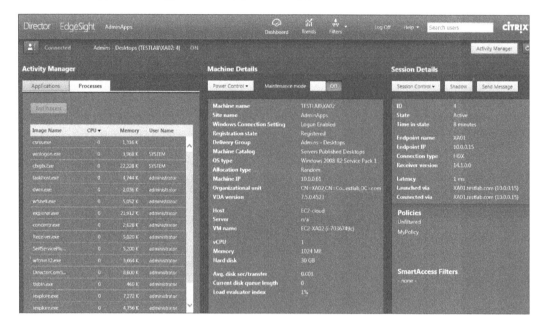

So, with the information and the granular details from this tool, administrators can easily diagnose any basic session launch- and performance-related issues.

Common XenDesktop® launch issues

When a user hits the StoreFront URL, his credentials are processed to present him with a list of published resources and multiple checks are performed in the background to select the correct virtual desktop to which the user must be connected.

In the whole VDA launch process, if any of the checkpoints or tests fail, the desktop launch is denied to the user and he is presented with an error on his screen. There are multiple events that can be presented to users who are facing launch refusal. The details of the events are presented in the following table:

Event Description	Explanation	Resolution
No desktop machine is available (Event 1101)	This event is generated when a user requests for a desktop launch to be assigned in a delivery group where no desktops are available to serve the request. There can be a reason why desktops are not available or are in maintenance mode.	As a resolution, you need to make sure that there are sufficient desktops available to serve the users. Either add more desktops to the desktop group using Citrix Studio or check and disable maintenance mode on the desktops.
Desktop machine refused connection (Event 1102)	The VDA agent actively refuses the connection request to make the machine ready for the user. This happens when the virtual desktop in question has not been configured with the right set of DDC controller servers.	Check the DDC list on the machine to resolve this issue.
Desktop machine sessions already active (Event 1103)	This error is reported when a user connection is disconnected and the session remains active; however, the reconnection has been configured to be disabled.	To allow active session reconnection, a registry entry `DisableActiveSessionReconnect` must be enabled. For details on how to create/modify registry entries for XenDesktop, please refer to the Citrix article at `http://support.citrix.com/article/CTX126704`.
Desktop machine in maintenance mode (Event 1105)	The machine that is requested to be launched is currently in maintenance mode.	You can launch Citrix Studio to check the status of the machine and disable maintenance mode to resolve the issue.
Requested protocol type is not supported (Event 1106)	This error is reported when a user tries to connect to a desktop on a protocol that is not supported; it can be RDP or any other protocol.	You can configure protocol restriction using the Broker PowerShell SDK using cmdlets for access policy rules.
Desktop machine already has a session (Event 1108)	The desktop that the user is trying to connect to is already running an active session. This happens when two users are assigned to the same desktop and one user already has a running session.	To resolve this issue, correct the desktop assignments.

Event Description	Explanation	Resolution
Desktop no longer available (Event 1109)	This event is reported when a desktop requested to be launched is no longer available; either it is disabled or deleted from Citrix Studio.	Launch Citrix Studio to check the status of the desktop and take corrective action to resolve this issue.
Machine start failures (Event 3012)	This event is reported when a XenDesktop is unable to start the machine on the hypervisor due to resources issue.	Check the hypervisor pool or cluster to make sure that it has enough resources to power on the machine.

Overcoming Citrix StoreFront™ port mapping issues

Every web server communication depends on two basic ports: 80 and 443. Citrix StoreFront is installed on a Windows server that has preinstalled IIS services. So, we have the option to configure our StoreFront server to communicate at port 80 for HTTP communication and 443 for HTTPS communication.

These are the two basic ports that you should take care of while configuring your firewall. The following figure is the basic flow diagram for Citrix StoreFront communication for the external access scenario:

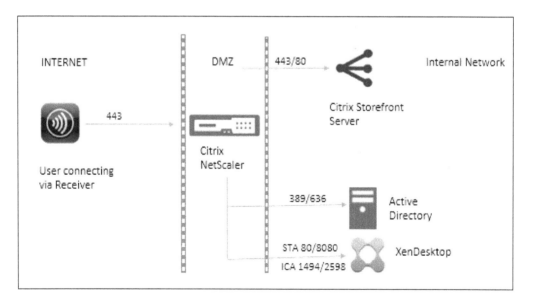

In this communication, users can receive multiple session launch errors due to incorrect firewall configuration for the required ports. We will discuss some basic session launch errors that users may encounter while launching desktop sessions.

- User gets the *incorrect username or password* error.

    There are multiple reasons for user authentication to fail. The following is the list of reasons relevant to the preceding communication flow diagram:

    ○ The authentication for users fails if there is a communication issue between NSIP or SNIP and domain controllers. Check your firewall configuration and make sure that your domain controller ports are open for successful communication with SNIP or NSIP.

    ○ There is an issue with the service account used for LDAP bind on the NetScaler LDAP vServer. The service account that you are using for LDAP binding should have the appropriate privileges.

    ○ Misconfigured base DN on the NetScaler LDAP vServer. You should always be careful to add the correct base DN when your users are vying for successful authentication.

    ○ Invalid credentials (the silliest and commonest scenario).

    To troubleshoot authentication on NetScaler, you can open NS shell and browse to the following path:

    ```
    >Shell
    ```

    Run the following command to change to the `tmp` directory:

    ```
    cd /tmp
    ```

    Run the following command to start the debugging process:

    ```
    Cat aaad.debug
    ```

 For more details on troubleshooting with the preceding commands, please refer to the Citrix article at http:// support.citrix.com/article/CTX114999.

- Cannot complete your request.

Following a successful authentication on NetScaler, this error is thrown to the users on the StoreFront web page. There are three very common areas that all Citrix administrators start exploring when they see this error.

- ° Is StoreFront able to resolve the FQDN of the callback URL on NetScaler?

  You should always be careful while configuring your remote access. Make sure that your StoreFront servers are able to reach the callback URL on NetScaler. We follow the best practice wherein we create a DNS alias entry for the VIP of NetScaler Gateway to FQDN to make it work smoothly.

  - ° The FQDN URL will be `https://remote.testlab.com`.
  - ° The VIP for the NetScaler Gateway vServer will be `10.100.1.15`.
  - ° A DNS entry (or localhost entry on the SF server) should be created: `remote.testlab.com` for IP address `10.100.1.15`.

- ° StoreFront server network connectivity or port issue with NetScaler Gateway vServer.

  For network connectivity, make sure that VIP of the NetScaler Gateway vServer is open for port `443` from the StoreFront server. Otherwise, StoreFront will throw the preceding error.

- ° StoreFront is not able to trust the SSL certificate of NetScaler Gateway.

  We have seen issues where the StoreFront server is not able to trust the SSL certificate and the SSL chain is broken; users often see this error. So, always make sure that your third-party SSL certificate, be it SAN/Wildcard or standard SSL, has a common name that matches your URL FQDN.

 Also, note that StoreFront doesn't trust a certificate that uses lower than 1024 bits encryption. So, always select an encryption higher than 1024 bits while generating a CSR request.

- • Unable to launch your application. Contact your helpdesk with following information: Cannot connect to Citrix XenApp server. Socket operation on non-socket.

This error is reported to users when NetScaler is not able to contact the Citrix STA servers on the XML port to validate the STA tickets or NetScaler is not able to reach the XenApp servers on ports 1494 and 2598. While configuring firewall rules for NetScaler to the backend infrastructure, we need to make sure that our Citrix STA and XenApp servers are reachable from NetScaler on the relevant ports.

For the best way to check whether the communication creates a service on NetScaler to point to your STA/XenApp servers on the relevant ports, refer to the following example service setup for the XenApp STA port:

Name	State	IP Address/Domain Name	Port	Protocol	Max Clients	Max Requests	Cache Type
XML_port_STA	Up	148.195.206.218	8080	TCP	0	0	SERVER

 For more details on how to configure a service and monitor it on NetScaler, visit the Citrix eDocs article at http://docs.citrix.com/en-us/netscaler/10-1.html.

Analyzing logs

Sometimes, it is difficult to isolate launch issues where you need to dig down by enabling logs to capture broker and VDA agent activities. You can start with the CDF trace for the following modules to capture the Citrix Broker Service traces:

- BrokerController
- Broker
- BrokerXmlServices
- BrokerControllerDAL
- BrokerDAL
- BrokerLicensing
- BrokerHostingManagement
- BrokerTicketStore
- BrokerHostingPlugin
- BrokerInterService
- PRODLIC_Library_Common
- PRODLIC_LicPolEng
- IcaClient_DesktopViewer

You can also enable Broker Service and VDA agent logs to do the analysis.

 To know more on how to enable and capture CDF, BrokerService, and VDA logs, please refer to *Chapter 2, Troubleshooting Toolkit for Citrix XenDesktop®*.

We will go through one example scenario to look at a step by step analysis. We will study and analyze one common desktop launch error: 1030.

Background

While connecting to the Citrix VDI, the user gets the famous error code 1030, as shown:

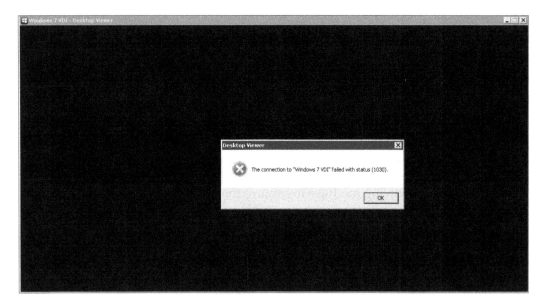

The error suggests that the communication didn't establish successfully on port 1494 or 2598 with the VDA machine and the connection timed out. This can be due to ports issue, DNS resolution, or IP conflicts.

Analysis steps

The steps for analysis are as follows:

1. On querying port results using Telnet from a client machine, we got a connection failure:

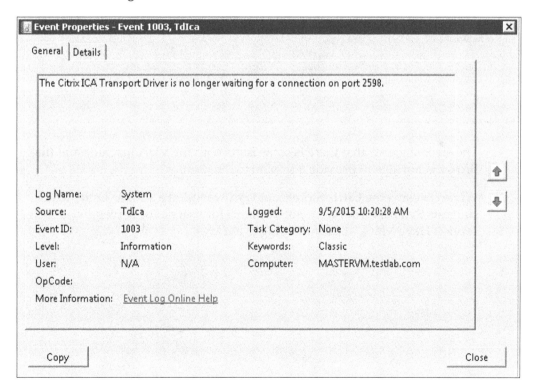

2. We started looking into the event viewer of the VDA machine. We didn't find any major errors; however, we found one informational event, which doesn't seem to be good. The event is as follows:

3. We went ahead and checked Delivery Controller logs and found the following event in application logs:

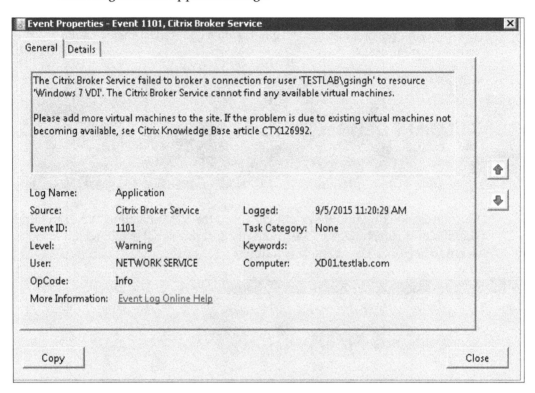

The error suggests that there is some issue with the VDA machine and the Broker is not able to provide a session to the users.

4. While checking the Citrix StoreFront logs, we found a similar issue, which suggests that resources were not available for users to be served by an XML service. Have a look at the following event logs:

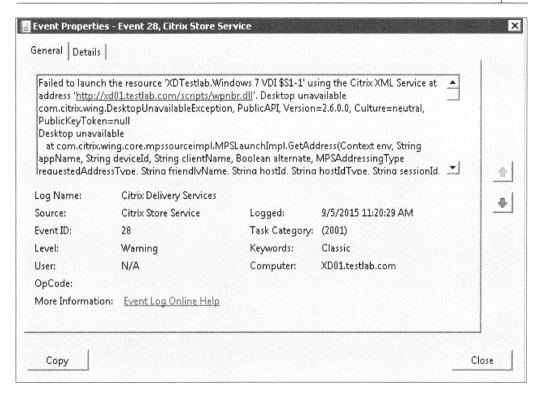

We checked the VDA machine and found that the Citrix Desktop service is running fine without any issue.

5. We enabled VDA agent logging on the VDA machine as the next step to troubleshoot this issue and also enabled Broker Service logging on the Delivery Controller.

The VDA agent log on the VDA machine: by analyzing the VDA agent logs on the VDA machine, we found that the Broker Agent (VDA agent) is timing out with highlighted message repeats, as shown here:

```
05/09/15 11:24:47.203 3280 5012: BrokerAgentMonitorManager:Monitor
ManagementAuditMethod - Waking up...
05/09/15 11:24:47.203 3280 5012: BrokerAgent:StackManager.
EnumerateSessionKeys: Enter
05/09/15 11:24:47.203 3280 5012: BrokerAgent:IsSimulationEnabled:
Simulated sessions are DISABLED
05/09/15 11:24:47.203 3280 5012: BrokerAgent:EnumerateSessionKeys
sessionKey = fb9d3ff3-05b4-4e23-a0dc-4731266438eb
05/09/15 11:24:47.203 3280 5012: BrokerAgent:EnumerateSessionKeys
sessionKey = a1f55c11-2443-49d5-85fe-efe066d74eea
```

```
05/09/15 11:24:47.218 3280 5012: BrokerAgentLaunchStore:LaunchStor
e:LaunchStoreCleanUp - 1 expired session key entries found
05/09/15 11:24:47.218 3280 5012: BrokerAgentLaunchStore:LaunchSto
re:LaunchStoreCleanUp - 1. Session Key: fb9d3ff3-05b4-4e23-a0dc-
4731266438eb, Launch Entries found: 1
05/09/15 11:24:47.218 3280 5012: BrokerAgentLaunchStore:LaunchS
tore:LaunchStoreCleanUp - Removing ticket hash from Ticket Hash
Dictionary
05/09/15 11:24:47.218 3280 5012: BrokerAgentLaunchStore:LaunchSto
re:LaunchStoreCleanUp - Removing launch ref hash from Launch Ref
Hash Dictionary
05/09/15 11:24:47.234 3280 5012: BrokerAgentLaunchStore:LaunchSto
re:LaunchStoreCleanUp - Removing session key fb9d3ff3-05b4-4e23-
a0dc-4731266438eb from Session Key Dictionary
05/09/15 11:24:57.841 3280 4368: BrokerAgentLoadBalancing:LoadMa
nagement CpuLoadRule:GetLoadIndex - This load rule is disabled.
Skipping index calculation.
05/09/15 11:25:27.853 3280 4368: BrokerAgent:AgentHeartBeatCB
Pv1_5.SendHeartbeatCbpV15Thread: Ping now. Max heartbeat exceeded.
```

Broker Service logs on the Delivery Controller didn't log any errors.

6. We took a CDF trace for the modules as explained in the last section. CDF tracing suggested that the ICA desktop viewer sessions are getting timed out and failing with error 1030:

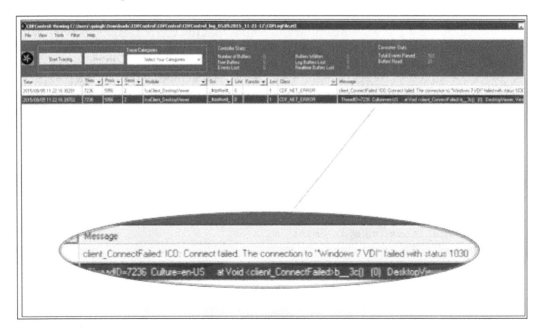

This analysis clearly explains that the sessions are getting timed out while the VDA machines are being contacted and there is something wrong with the communication that happens on port 2598.

7. We checked our firewall rules and found that there is no block configured for this particular VDA machine.

Resolution

Ultimately, the issue was found with the ICA-TCP listener on the VDA machine that was not responding and hence causing timeouts (Windows 2008 R2 Server OS VDA). We recreated the ICA-TCP listener to resolve this issue.

 You can recreate ICA-TCP listeners using the built-in remote desktop services configuration utility. To create a new remote desktop service connection using an RDP or ICA listener, you can follow the steps outlined in the MS article at https://technet.microsoft.com/en-us/library/cc771694.aspx.

Summary

We now have a good understanding of the VDA launch process and the skills acquired in this chapter will enable us to troubleshoot any kind of Citrix VDA launch issue that comes up in our XenDesktop environment.

In our next chapter, we will focus on the Citrix XenDesktop services architecture and its related issues.

6

Surpassing XenDesktop® Service Issues

In the last chapter, we discussed the VDA launch process, the communication framework, common issues, and the difficulties one can encounter while troubleshooting and resolving issues related to VDA sessions. We will now focus on the XenDesktop Services architecture; every administrator who is keen on developing a good understanding of the troubleshooting skills required for XenDesktop Services related issues must know this.

The ultimate goal of this chapter is to explain XenDesktop Service architecture and develop essential skills required to troubleshoot any service-related issue arising in your XenDesktop environment.

In this chapter, we will cover the following points:

- Understanding the XenDesktop service architecture
- Enabling service logs
- Surpassing database account credential issues
- Verifying Active Directory integration
- Using PowerShell to check the status of services

Understanding the XenDesktop® service architecture

XenDesktop works on the FMA architecture, which includes subsets of multiple services that are responsible for the entire communication flow from controllers to VDAs for a successful desktop delivery platform.

To understand the communication flow and how the services interact with each other, refer to the following flow diagram that is based on the FMA service architecture. It includes 10-12 primary services that build up the complete FMA architecture.

There are 10 controller-level services with two services that run on a VDA device; we will discuss all the services and their roles in the following flow chart:

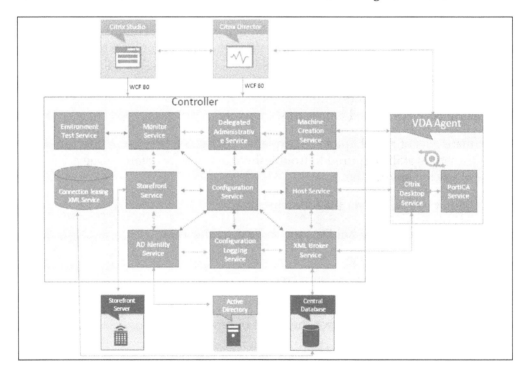

To understand this illustration and each service role in the communication framework, we have listed down the service interaction and roles, as follows:

- **Broker Service (XML)**: This is one of the most common and important services, responsible to broker new sessions, desktop enumeration, STA tickets, handling and managing session data, and so on. This service interacts with the Desktop Service on the VDA to manage all the communication, to and fro from Delivery Controller to VDA.

- **Configuration Service**: This service stores the configuration for all the services in this framework, so each service needs to register its status on startup with this service. This is considered to be one of the critical services in the XenDesktop Services architecture.

- **AD ID Identity Service**: This manages all the Active Directory computer accounts for XenApp and XenDesktop machines.

- **Configuration Logging Service**: As the name suggests, this service is responsible for logging all the configuration changes within the XenDesktop site. This includes all the administrative changes being made in the environment.

- **Delegated Administration Service**: This service is responsible for managing all the administration and configuration for all the delegated administrative permissions. If the service goes down, you can't modify the existing or add any new administrative accounts.

- **Machine Creation Service**: This service is responsible for the creation of new virtual machines If this service fails or goes unresponsive, no new virtual machine creation will be possible.

 If you are looking to scale up your virtual infrastructure or serve physical machines lying in your datacentre, you should implement Citrix **Provisioning Services** (**PVS**)

- **Citrix Host Service**: This service is responsible for managing connections between hypervisor and delivery controller.

- **Environment Test Service**: This service conducts and manages all tests on your XenDesktop site. You can initiate and validate the tests from Citrix Studio.

- **Monitor Service**: This service is responsible for monitoring all the FMA architecture and generates specific alerts for the issues found in the XenDesktop site. Make a note, that although this service is capable of generating alerts and warnings to alert you that something is wrong within your environment, it doesn't pinpoint the exact problem within your XenDesktop site and where you need to start investigating to resolve the problem.

 The best place to start the investigation related to XenDesktop services is to fire a PowerShell window and begin issuing commands related to each service. Please refer *Chapter 2, Troubleshooting Toolkit for Citrix XenDesktop®*, for details on checking the status of each service to troubleshoot service-related issues.

- **StoreFront™ Service**: This service manages Storefront deployment. You also have an option to manage Storefront configuration from Citrix Studio.

- **Citrix Desktop Service**: This is one of the two major services running on your VDA, this service interacts with Delivery Controller and the PortICA service to exchange information related to logon ticket data and user credentials for authentication and STA ticket validation.

- **The PortICA Service or PicaSvc2.exe**: This is the other service running on VDA, this service accepts the initial connection requests and locks the workstation. It communicates with the display driver to change the remote display of the remote desktop, the information is passed on to the Thinwire driver, which then communicates with the Desktop Service.

Enabling service logs

Service based logging can be enabled via the command line or using Citrix Scout installed by default on XenDesktop 7.5 and later versions. Citrix Scout lacks some feature logging; it doesn't enable Citrix Broker Service agent logging.

So, it's always better to enable your environment's service-based logging using the command line.

An example of a command to enable Citrix Broker Service Log is as follows:

```
BrokerService.exe -Logfile "C:\XDLogs\Citrix Broker Service.log"
```

You need to run this command from the CMD prompt while you are in the appropriate service directory, such as `C:\Program Files\ Citrix\Citrix Broker Service\Service`.

Surpassing database account credential issues

The XenDesktop site central-database is accessed by the services running on each controller. These services' access to the database is controlled by Active Directory machine accounts. The controller machine accounts and users are provided sufficient minimum database access privileges to carry out the daily operations.

Using machine accounts presents a simple and secure model to safeguard critical data in XenDesktop database. However, there are some administrative operations that fall out of scope for these machine accounts' access privileges and in those scenarios, we need to ask the database administrator with elevated privileges to pitch in and perform the tasks via SQL scripts.

The database access flow diagram is as follows:

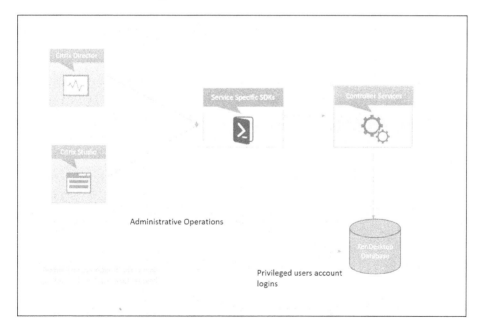

The XenDesktop service doesn't support use of SQL authentication. This is due to the fact that SQL scripts and SDKs are based on machine account logons and using SQL authentication can expose the SQL passwords through the SDKs.

Each XenDesktop service connects with the database using the controller's machine accounts. Citrix Studio, Director and PowerShell SDKs connect to the database using one of the services and their machine account login. There are no separate logins required for these components.

 To know and configure the right set of XenDesktop database and administrative permissions, please refer to the Citrix knowledgebase article at `http://support.citrix.com/article/CTX127998`.

If the permissions are not set correctly, you may encounter issues related to database permissions while configuring or modifying a XenDesktop site.

There can be situations where you can still see the **Insufficient privileges** error while configuring your XenDesktop site database, even after following the recommended permissions given here.

In order to start your troubleshooting, you should always begin with network connectivity:

1. The first step should be to check if the database server is reachable and the firewall has been configured to allow DB ports TCP: `1433`, TCP: `1434`, and UDP: `1434`.

2. To test the ports, you can always use Telnet to verify if the ports are opened or not.

3. Once you have established that the database server is reachable and the relevant ports are open on the firewall, you should check the permissions on the XenDesktop site database by contacting your SQL team; it should be configured as per recommendations given in the Citrix Article CTX127998 (`http://support.citrix.com/article/CTX127998`).

Active Directory integration

XenDesktop relies on Active Directory for its operations. AD provides a data store that stores information related to users, computers, services, and other objects. The Delivery Controller and VDA depend upon the AD to establish trust relationships to secure communication.

XenDesktop controllers and VDA use AD for a number of tasks, such as:

- **Authentication**: End users authenticate to DDC and VDA using Active Directory

- **Management console authentication**: Administrators authenticate to DDC using AD credentials to make any changes to the XenDesktop site

- **Kerberos**: DDC and VDAs use the Kerberos security feature provided by AD to establish secure and encrypted communication channel

- **Controller Discovery using Active Directory**: Virtual desktops in a XenDesktop environment need to register themselves with the Controller server to be managed by a broker and allow ICA connections from client devices. One of the configuration methods for this discovery can be done by Active Directory. Citrix provides a built-in setup script to enable this configuration. The script can be located on the XenDesktop Controller server under the path `C:\Program Files\Citrix\Broker\Service\Setup Scripts\Set-ADControllerDiscovery.Ps1`.

> This method is deprecated and no more used for XenDesktop 7.x controllers and is just recommended for backwards compatibility.
>
> Please refer to the Citrix article at `http://support.citrix.com/article/ctx122417/` to know more on supported Active Directory configuration for XenDesktop infrastructure.

Using PowerShell to check the status of services

There can be situations where you won't be able to isolate issues related to services by looking at the alerts generated by Director or event viewer. To isolate issues related to XenDesktop services, you can always check the status of services using PowerShell commands.

Here are a few example cmdlets to check the status of important FMA services:

- `Get-BrokerServiceStatus`
- `Get-ConfigServiceStatus`
- `Get-HypServiceStatus`
- `Get-AcctServiceStatus`
- `Get-ProvServiceStatus`

It is recommended to create a personal PowerShell profile to troubleshoot service-related issues. We discussed how to create a PoSH profile in *Chapter 2, Troubleshooting Toolkit for Citrix XenDesktop®*.

 You can also import the XenDesktop PowerShell module by issuing the `Add-PSSnapin Citrix*` command; it is not necessary to create a PoSH profile to take advantage of PowerShell in a XenDesktop environment.

The listed cmdlets will give you the state of the service and whether it is running or not. This looks similar to the status you view in the Services snap-in on the Windows server. However, it should be noted that. when there is any issue with any of the FMA services, these commands will give you a valid reason for the failure of service communication. Let's have a look at the following screenshot:

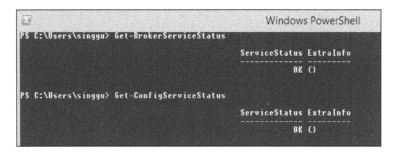

As shown in the preceding example cmdlets, the service status returned to us is **OK**, which means that the service is connected to the database and is running fine.

If there is any issue with your FMA services, you might receive errors as described here:

- **DbUnconfigured**: This means that the service doesn't have a database connection configured.

- **DBRejectedConnection**: This means that the database rejected the logon from the service. This may be because of bad credentials or database is not installed.

- **DBNotFound**: This means that the DB could not be located with the configured connection string.

- **PendingFailure**: This means that the connectivity between DB and service is lost.

- **DBMissingOptionalFeature**: This suggests that the service connected to the DB is valid but it doesn't seems to have the full functionality required for optimal performance. A database upgrade is advisable.

 You can see a complete list of all possible return values by issuing the `Help` command as shown here:

`Help Get-BrokerServiceStatus -Full`

So, on receiving any of the *non-ok* return codes, you can check the description of the return code by issuing the command as explained here and troubleshoot the underlying problem.

Summary

We now have a good understanding of the XenDesktop service-oriented FMA architecture. The skills learned in this chapter will enable administrators to troubleshoot any XenDesktop service-related issues.

In our next chapter, we will focus on troubleshooting performance issues related to a XenDesktop environment

Troubleshooting Performance

7

In our last chapter, we discussed the XenDesktop services architecture, the communication flow between XenDesktop services, common issues, and the difficulties one can encounter while troubleshooting and resolving services related issues. We will now focus on troubleshooting performance issues related to the XenDesktop infrastructure. Troubleshooting and resolving performance issues can become a nightmare for administrators if they are not diagnosed with the right approach.

The ultimate goal of this chapter is to understand the basics of performance parameters, details of sizing for the environment, and troubleshooting performance issues using Citrix and third-party tools.

In this chapter, we will cover the following topics:

- Getting a grip on the performance parameters
- Understanding sizing requirements
- Capturing performance data — working with Perfmon, QSlice, and Process Explorer
- Using Xperf or Windows Performance Analyzer

Getting a grip on the performance parameters

We see companies spend lot of money on building the base infrastructure, purchasing software, networking, storage, and computing to build a better and stable VDI solution to meet the demands of their user bases.

However, the main key area or weak point lies in the organization's effective monitoring solution. This happens because many customers think that the budget or cost involved in purchasing such monitoring solutions doesn't really make any sense or affect their stable running environment.

So, many customers choose scripts and automated performance counters on the servers to capture basic performance parameters such as CPU, memory, disk utilization, and so on. These basic performance metrics and collected data help customers to analyze high-level performance metrics, but they do not provide a complete monitoring solution to integrate every layer of performance metric needed.

Let's discuss the basic performance parameters that are necessary and recommended by Citrix for a basic monitoring solution:

Performance Metric	Description	Remediation
Processor: % processor time	% processor is the percentage of elapsed time that the processor takes to process a non-idle thread. This is the primary indicator of processor activity and displays the average percentage of busy time during the sample interval for which the data is taken.	For the purpose of troubleshooting and remediation, we need to identify the processes that consume more processor time. This can be monitored by using the Windows Task Manager or resource monitor or by configuring the Perfmon counters.
System: processor queue length	This measures the number of threads in the processor queue. It captures only ready threads and not the running threads. There is a single queue for all processors, even for servers with multiple processors. So, for multiple processors, you need to divide the number of threads by number of processors. Processor queue length is considered to be sustainably good if the number falls below 10 per processor.	CPU bottleneck can be identified by a long queue number.
Memory: available MBs	This indicates the amount of available memory left in the system after non-paged pool, paged pool, processes working set, and filesystem cache have consumed their share.	We need to identify the processes or services that consume more memory and take corrective actions to resolve the issue.

Performance Metric	Description	Remediation
Memory: pages/ seconds	This indicates the rate at which pages are read and written back on the disk.	A memory bottleneck is caused by a high value reported by this counter. Ideally, the value should be < 10.
Paging file: % usage	This indicates the percentage usage of page file utilization.	The value should be monitored carefully in conjunction with pages/sec and available memory left in the system.
Logical/ physical disk: % free space	This indicates the percentage of free space left on the logical disk to be utilized.	Disk cleaning activities.
Logical/ physical disk: % disk time	This indicates how much of the disk is busy in processing R/W requests.	If you notice a high percentage of disk time for multiple processes, you should think about upgrading your disk system.
Logical/ physical disk: current queue length	This measures the disk congestion.	A long disk queue length indicates a performance bottleneck for the disk. The ideal number should be <= 1 per spindle consistency. This can be caused by high number of disk I/Os or due to smaller physical memory allocated to the system.
Logical/ physical disk: avg. disk sec/ read, avg. disk sec/ write, and avg. disk sec/ transfer	This indicates the average time, in seconds, for a disk to read/write/ transfer to and from a disk.	High disk read or write value indicates a disk performance bottleneck. The ideal value should be <= 15ms.
Network interface: total bytes/sec	This is the rate at which the network interface card processes network bytes.	The ideal value should be > 8MB/s for a 100 Mbits/s adapter and > 80MB/s for a 1000 Mbits/s adapter.

We discussed XenDesktop counters in *Chapter 2, Troubleshooting Toolkit for Citrix XenDesktop®*, which can be of great help while configuring Perfmon counters for XenDesktop.

Understanding sizing requirements

Performance bottleneck of any infrastructure is linked directly to the sizing of its base infrastructure components. So, it's very important to ensure that any new environment that is being designed is built efficiently using proper sizing guidelines.

In this section, we will cover the basic sizing requirements of a XenDesktop environment, which is the key for a successful deployment.

For any XenDesktop deployment, you need to work on sizing the following components:

- Number of infrastructure servers
- vRAM and vCPU requirements for the infrastructure servers
- vRAM and vCPU requirements for VMs
- Base hardware required for the hypervisor layer
- SQL databases
- Storage
- IOPS requirements
- Bandwidth requirements
- vGPU and HDX 3D Pro sizing

Earlier, we sized the environment based on the data captured by enabling Perfmon counters on the VDI/server to measure the concurrent user load, memory/CPU stats, IOPS calculation, and so on. The method is still relevant and is used by many administrators for sizing smaller deployments.

Citrix has provided a wonderful online tool called Citrix Project Accelerator to perform sizing on your XenApp, XenClient, and XenDesktop environment. This tool was designed by Citrix Consulting after thorough testing. You only need Citrix account credentials to get started with this tool.

To get started with Citrix Project Accelerator, please visit `http://project.citrix.com/`.

You need to create a new project to get started with the tool and follow the framework to define your organization's needs and requirements:

The tool allows you to start from scratch and follow best practices and recommendations for hardware sizing, storage, networking, user groups and applications to structure a complete architecture design for your deployment.

Project Accelerator is structured in three phases:

1. Assess
2. Design
3. Deploy

The assessment phase

In the assessment phase, you need to define and assess the organizational requirements starting from the organization's priorities, number of concurrent users, user group type, applications, licensing and infrastructure building blocks:

The design phase

The design phase gives you a solid foundation for sizing storage, calculating IOPS, memory/CPU's sizing, network throughput and configuring remote access. If you assess your organization's requirements and follow the recommended design properly, Project Accelerator will give you what is needed and take away all your worries.

Let's have a look at the following customized architecture diagram generated by XenDesktop Project Accelerator. It provides you with the complete details about sizing your infrastructure components, IOPS calculations, and VDI requirements.

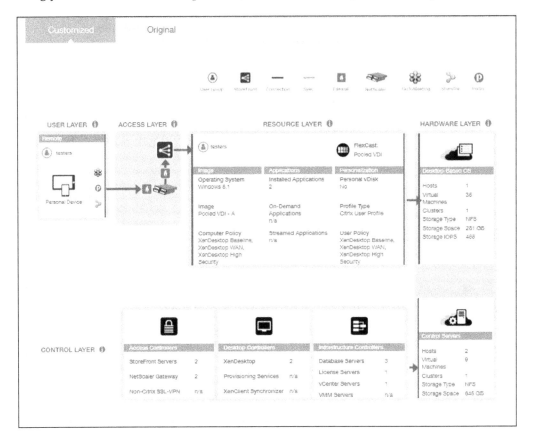

The deployment phase

In the deployment phase, you only need to follow the sizing guidelines and architecture diagram created by Project Accelerator to successfully complete your deployment.

There are other third-party tools available to do the sizing for your VDI deployment. The sizing calculators that I like the most were developed by Andrzej Gołębiowski. It fulfils your requirements and provides you with all the sizing details for your VDI project:

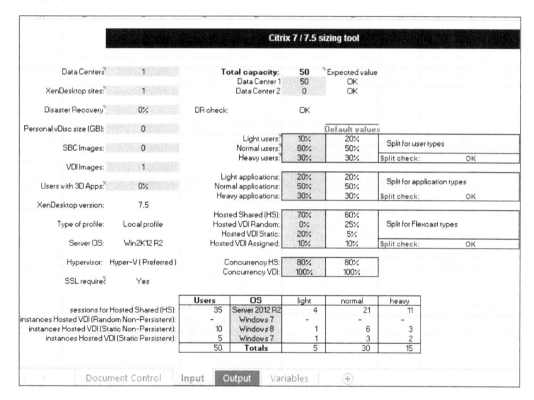

 To download this wonderful tool, you can visit `http://blog.citrix24.com/Xendesktop7_Sizing_Calculator.`

NVIDIA provides GRID vGPU, which is a feature of Kepler-based GPUs that allows hardware level virtualization of the GPU. Citrix was the first to provide the Citrix HDX 3D Pro solution to support this capability in the year 2013 and Citrix XenServer was the only hypervisor to support GRID vGPU. Recently, vSphere 6 added support to join the group.

The sizing and understanding of the NVIDIA GRID vGPU architecture for XenDesktop with HDX 3D Pro is out of scope for this book. However, I recommend you to read the following design and reviewer guides to understand the deployment, design, and sizing requirements:

- `https://www.citrix.com/content/dam/citrix/en_us/documents/products-solutions/virtualize-3d-professional-graphics-design-guide.pdf`
- `https://www.citrix.com/content/dam/citrix/en_us/documents/go/reviewers-guide-remote-3d-graphics-apps-part-1-xenserver-gpu-passthrough.pdf`
- `http://www.citrix.com/content/dam/citrix/en_us/documents/go/reviewers-guide-remote-3d-graphics-apps-part-3-xenserver-vgpu.pdf`
- `http://www.citrix.com/content/dam/citrix/en_us/documents/go/reviewers-guide-remote-3d-graphics-apps-part-2-vsphere-gpu-passthrough.pdf`
- `http://www.citrix.com/content/dam/citrix/en_us/documents/products-solutions/reviewers-guide-for-hdx-3d-pro.pdf`

Capturing performance data

Much advancement has been made in the XenDesktop product suite and Citrix Director to capture data and present it through EdgeSight. However, these tools don't capture or provide bottleneck issues related to network and storage layers. Administrators have to work with multiple teams to perform analysis to understand if there is any bottleneck in the network and storage components that is slowing things up for the XenDesktop performance.

Performance Monitor

To troubleshoot performance issues, many administrators take help from a very old and powerful Windows tool called Performance Monitor. You can configure custom control sets in order to monitor multiple components for a XenDesktop site. It may be configured to monitor basic components, such as CPU/memory, disk utilization for read and writes, disk/storage IOPS, SQL database counters, and other relevant counters.

 To learn more about configuring Performance Monitor counters, please refer to *Chapter 2, Troubleshooting Toolkit for Citrix XenDesktop®*.

QSlice or Process Monitor

Since the era of Windows 2000 systems, Microsoft has provided a very good tool to analyze CPU performance. Task Manager displays CPU usage by value and to view the information graphically, administrators used to prefer QuickSlice (`Qslice.exe`), which is found in Windows 2000 Resource Kit tools. This tool was later replaced by Process Explorer and Procmon.

The basic configuration of setting and capturing the process, registry, filesystem, and network related data with Procmon has already been explained in *Chapter 2, Troubleshooting Toolkit for Citrix XenDesktop®*. Go though it once to configure Process Monitor to capture performance.

Xperf or Windows Performance Analyzer

Windows Performance Analyzer has been an excellent tool to analyze any performance related issues. Many administrators rely on this to troubleshoot slow logon issues in XenApp/XenDesktop environment.

 Refer to *Chapter 2, Troubleshooting Toolkit for Citrix XenDesktop®*, for details on how to configure and troubleshoot performance issues in your XenDesktop environment.

Case study – troubleshooting a slow logon

Problem

Users reported that they are experiencing a slow logon where it takes more than a minute to log into Citrix Desktop.

Environment

The following is the summary provided for customer's Citrix environment:

- XenDesktop 7.6
- Citrix Profile Management 5.2.1
- Citrix ICA Client 14.2.0.10

Troubleshooting

We found that all the users were experiencing delays between 55 seconds to 90 seconds while logging into Citrix Desktop.

We started troubleshooting using Citrix Director; we found that logging into a Citrix desktop took 59 seconds, which wasn't that bad. However, a customer complained that it was pretty fast a month back:

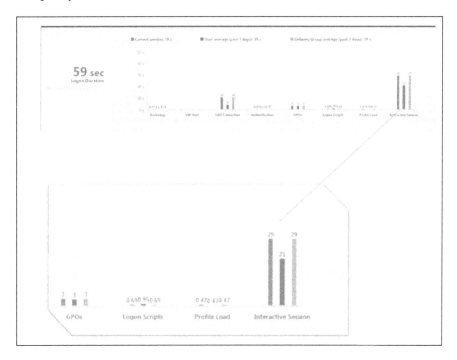

Citrix Director provides the granular details of the logon process with the duration. We found that interactive sessions took more than 29 seconds and this was consistent for all user logons.

 An interactive session is a logon process duration, which hands off the keyboard and mouse control to the user.

We took a Procmon trace to understand what is going on for 29 seconds, which is delaying the logon. After applying the filter with session ID for the user, together with the `winlogon.exe` process, we found a huge amount of *Access Denied* entries for the backup client and Internet settings zone maps. See the following screen capture from the Procmon trace:

Process Name	Operation	Path	Result
CvSystemTray.exe	CreateFile	C:\Windows\Temp\Commvault Systems\LogFiles\CvSystemTray.log	ACCESS DENIED
CvSystemTray.exe	CreateFile	C:\Windows\Temp\Commvault Systems\LogFiles\CvSystemTray.log	ACCESS DENIED
CvSystemTray.exe	CreateFile	C:\Windows\Temp\Commvault Systems\LogFiles\CvSystemTray.log	ACCESS DENIED
CvSystemTray.exe	CreateFile	C:\Windows\Temp\Commvault Systems\LogFiles\CvSystemTray.log	ACCESS DENIED
concentr.exe	RegOpenKey	HKLM\System\CurrentControlSet\Services\WinSock2\Parameters	ACCESS DENIED
concentr.exe	RegOpenKey	HKLM\System\CurrentControlSet\Services\WinSock2\Parameters	ACCESS DENIED
Win7LookAndFeel..	RegOpenKey	HKLM\System\CurrentControlSet\services\eventlog\Security	ACCESS DENIED
CvSystemTray.exe	CreateFile	C:\Windows\Temp\Commvault Systems\LogFiles\CvSystemTray.log	ACCESS DENIED
CvSystemTray.exe	CreateFile	C:\Windows\Temp\Commvault Systems\LogFiles\CvSystemTray.log	ACCESS DENIED
Win7LookAndFeel..	RegOpenKey	HKLM\System\CurrentControlSet\services\eventlog\Security	ACCESS DENIED
Win7LookAndFeel..	RegOpenKey	HKLM\System\CurrentControlSet\services\eventlog\Security	ACCESS DENIED
Win7LookAndFeel..	RegOpenKey	HKLM\System\CurrentControlSet\services\eventlog\Security	ACCESS DENIED
concentr.exe	RegOpenKey	HKLM\Software\Wow6432Node\Microsoft\Windows\CurrentVersion\Internet Settings\ZoneMap\	ACCESS DENIED
concentr.exe	RegOpenKey	HKLM\Software\Wow6432Node\Microsoft\Windows\CurrentVersion\Internet Settings\ZoneMap\	ACCESS DENIED
concentr.exe	RegOpenKey	HKLM\Software\Wow6432Node\Microsoft\Windows\CurrentVersion\Internet Settings\ZoneMap\	ACCESS DENIED
concentr.exe	RegOpenKey	HKLM\Software\Wow6432Node\Microsoft\Windows\CurrentVersion\Internet Settings\ZoneMap\	ACCESS DENIED
CvSystemTray.exe	CreateFile	C:\Windows\Temp\Commvault Systems\LogFiles\CvSystemTray.log	ACCESS DENIED
CvSystemTray.exe	CreateFile	C:\Windows\Temp\Commvault Systems\LogFiles\CvSystemTray.log	ACCESS DENIED
CvSystemTray.exe	CreateFile	C:\Windows\Temp\Commvault Systems\LogFiles\CvSystemTray.log	ACCESS DENIED
Receiver.exe	RegOpenKey	HKLM\System\CurrentControlSet\Services\WinSock2\Parameters	ACCESS DENIED
Receiver.exe	RegOpenKey	HKLM\System\CurrentControlSet\Services\WinSock2\Parameters	ACCESS DENIED
CvSystemTray.exe	CreateFile	C:\Windows\Temp\Commvault Systems\LogFiles\CvSystemTray.log	ACCESS DENIED
CvSystemTray.exe	CreateFile	C:\Windows\Temp\Commvault Systems\LogFiles\CvSystemTray.log	ACCESS DENIED
CvSystemTray.exe	CreateFile	C:\Windows\Temp\Commvault Systems\LogFiles\CvSystemTray.log	ACCESS DENIED
Receiver.exe	RegCreateKey	HKLM\Software\Wow6432Node\Citrix\Receiver\Inventory\Services	ACCESS DENIED
Receiver.exe	RegCreateKey	HKLM\SOFTWARE\Wow6432Node\Citrix\Receiver\Inventory\Services	ACCESS DENIED
CvSystemTray.exe	CreateFile	C:\Windows\Temp\Commvault Systems\LogFiles\CvSystemTray.log	ACCESS DENIED
CvSystemTray.exe	CreateFile	C:\Windows\Temp\Commvault Systems\LogFiles\CvSystemTray.log	ACCESS DENIED
CvSystemTray.exe	CreateFile	C:\Windows\Temp\Commvault Systems\LogFiles\CvSystemTray.log	ACCESS DENIED
taskhost.exe	RegOpenKey	HKLM\Software\Microsoft\Windows\CurrentVersion\Internet Settings\5.0\Cache\Content	ACCESS DENIED
CvSystemTray.exe	CreateFile	C:\Windows\Temp\Commvault Systems\LogFiles\CvSystemTray.log	ACCESS DENIED
CvSystemTray.exe	CreateFile	C:\Windows\Temp\Commvault Systems\LogFiles\CvSystemTray.log	ACCESS DENIED
Receiver.exe	RegOpenKey	HKLM\Software\Wow6432Node\Microsoft\Windows\CurrentVersion\Internet Settings\ZoneMap\	ACCESS DENIED
Receiver.exe	RegOpenKey	HKLM\Software\Wow6432Node\Microsoft\Windows\CurrentVersion\Internet Settings\ZoneMap\	ACCESS DENIED

 For details on how to take a Procmon trace, refer to *Chapter 2, Troubleshooting Toolkit for Citrix XenDesktop®*.

This issue directed us to look for the GPOs, where Internet settings are being pushed to diagnose the issue. We found that the customer had a domain-wide user policy that was pushing all the Internet settings and was also responsible for setting the desktop wallpaper on the desktops.

We enabled WMI filtering to apply the policy to Windows 7 desktop operating systems only, for the purpose of testing this on the server VDA published desktops. Surprisingly, it reduced our interactive session time from 29 seconds to 7 seconds. Refer the following screenshot:

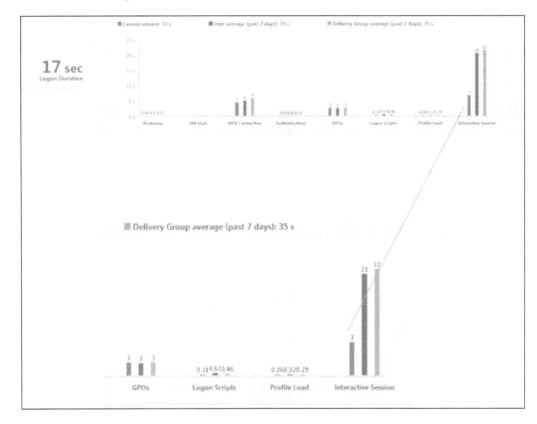

Resolution

There were multiple Internet settings that required correct permissions on the following registry paths:

- `HKLM\Software\Wow6432Node\Microsoft\Windows\CurrentVersion\`
  `Internet Settings\ZoneMap\`
- `HKLM\Software\Microsoft\Windows\CurrentVersion\Internet`
  `Settings\ZoneMap\`

Also, we fixed the bitmap image of the desktop wallpaper that was taking a little longer to apply.

 A more granular study for the Winlogon process can be done using Xperf or Windows Performance Analyzer. You can refer to *Chapter 2, Troubleshooting Toolkit for Citrix XenDesktop®*, for the tool's usage.

Summary

We now have a good understanding of performance analysis and the tools required to troubleshoot any performance related issues surfacing in a XenDesktop environment.

In the next chapter, we will focus on troubleshooting printing issues related to the XenDesktop environment.

8
Solving Printing Issues

In the last chapter, we discussed the basics of performance parameters, details of sizing for environment, and troubleshooting performance issues using Citrix and third-party tools.

We will now discuss the basic printing issues that might arise in XenDesktop infrastructure for users. Printing issues are the most common and frustrating for administrators to troubleshoot, if they are not tackled with the right approach.

The ultimate goal of this chapter is to understand the basics of setting up the Citrix printing architecture, configuring printing policies, and troubleshooting printing issues.

In this chapter, we will cover the following points:

- Understanding the printing setup
- Citrix printing policies
- Exploring the XenDesktop printing registry settings
- Using Print Detective and StressPrinters

Understanding the printing setup

Citrix XenDesktop supports a variety of printing solutions. Before choosing any solution for printing, we must understand the organization's needs and the solution that offers to meet the desired requirement.

The following are the solutions that are supported by Citrix XenApp and XenDesktop: let's have a quick look at what each solution offers.

Provisioning printers

The process by which printers are created in XenApp or XenDesktop sessions is called **printer provisioning**. Printer provisioning is classified into two types:

- **Static**: In this type of provisioning, a collection of printers is created in every session. This type of printer collection is created each time and does not vary as per policy. This is best suited for smaller setups.

- **Dynamic**: In this type of provisioning, a collection of printers is created in each session according to policies. Here, the set of printers created might vary in each session based on the policy changes, IP subnet, or user location base. This is best suited for geographically widespread enterprise environments.

Many organizations choose **hybrid** provisioning to map some static printers to each employee's login along with some specific printers whose mapping is restricted to a set of employees controlled via Active Directory groups.

Auto-creation is a type of dynamic provisioning and every Citrix administrator might have used it in his XenApp/XenDesktop setup. It creates all printers attached to a client device—local printers as well as network printers.

It is not necessary to map all the printers for all users in their user sessions. So, this can be controlled via the following Citrix policies:

- **Auto-create all client printers**: This is the default setting
- **Do not auto-create all client printers**: This turns off printer auto-creation, users need to manually add printers in their ICA sessions
- **Auto-create client default printers only**: This only creates a printer that is directly configured as a default printer on a client device
- **Auto-create local printers only**: This only creates local printers directly connected to the client device using the LPT, COM, USB, and TCP ports

 Never choose the **Auto-create all client printers** option; it can significantly increase session logon time as each printer is enumerated during the logon process.

Session printers

Session printers are a collection of network based printers created using a Citrix policy during each session logon. These can be statically or dynamically provisioned depending upon the Citrix policy configuration.

The session printers can behave as static printers, if configured to be mapped in each session for all users and can vary as well if a filter is applied using the IP subnet or user groups.

Print driver management

Print driver management is the most tedious work in a XenApp/XenDesktop environment where hundreds of printers need to be managed. There are several methods available to manage print drivers.

Automatic installation

When a user connects to a XenApp/XenDesktop session, a check is performed to validate whether the required printer driver is installed in the operating system. If this check fails, a native printer driver installation will trigger automatically. Otherwise, Citrix Universal Print Driver will be used instead.

If there are mobile users who roam regularly and access printers from multiple devices and locations, they can cause inconsistency across sessions as they may access different resources each time they connect to a XenApp or XenDesktop session. It becomes very challenging to troubleshoot printing problems in this type of scenario due to the multiple sets of drivers that are installed on hosted devices.

[It is always recommended to not enable automatic installation of native drivers to ensure consistency and avoid printing issues.]

Manual installation

There can be scenarios where native drivers are not available and Citrix Universal Print Driver is not supported for specific printer models. In this case, you can install the printer drivers manually. However, this can again be a challenge for users using multiple devices and different locations to access printers, and manual installation of the print drivers can cause inconsistency in the environment. It is always recommended to install print drivers on the master image to ensure consistency.

Citrix Universal Print Driver

Citrix **Universal Print Driver** (UPD) is an independent print driver and has been designed to work with most of the printer models. It simplifies printer driver management and administration tasks. Citrix UPD consists of two components:

- **Server component**: The Citrix UPD is installed along with the XenApp or XenDesktop VDA installation. When a user initiates a print job, the UPD driver records the output and sends it across to the endpoint device via HDX.

- **Client component**: The Citrix UPD is installed with the Citrix Receiver installation. It fetches the incoming stream from the server component and forwards it to the local printing subsystem, where the print job is actually rendered using device-specific print drivers.

Vendor-specific print drivers

There are multiple vendors who provide vendor-specific universal print drivers to simplify print driver management. So, you can also use a vendor-specific universal driver, which can help you reduce the number of print drivers to be managed across XenApp or XenDesktop devices.

It is always recommended to install a vendor-specific universal driver on the master image for XenApp and XenDesktop.

Citrix Universal Print Server

Citrix introduced the Citrix Universal Print Server to extend its support for universal printing to network printers. It comprises of two components:

- **Server component**: The Citrix UPS component is installed on a Windows based print server. It captures the print data and forwards it to the respective printer using the Citrix UPServer virtual port monitor.

- **Client component**: The client component is installed on the base image of the XenApp server or XenDesktop Windows operating system. It captures the EMF- or XPS-based print stream from the Citrix UPD driver and forwards it to the print server. Print commands and print data are sent to their respective ports.

Print commands are sent over TCP port 8080 and print data is sent over TCP port 7229 by default.

Citrix printing policies

Printer mappings are controlled by Citrix policies in a Citrix XenApp or XenDesktop environment. It is very important to configure these policies correctly in your XenDesktop environment, to avoid any unusual hiccups and issues.

Let's have a look at the major Citrix printing policies that every administrator must know about and more essentially, they should know where to apply them.

Auto-create client printers

The Auto-create client printers policy is one of the most important and basic policies that is used in a XenApp or XenDesktop environment. The policy can be configured in four ways:

- **Auto-create all client printers**: This setting will allow the auto-creation of all client printers on the client device, be it locally attached printers on the client device or the network mapped printers.

- **Auto-create client default printer only**: This setting will allow auto-creation of the client's default printer only. None of the other printers will be auto-created in the ICA session.

- **Auto-create all local (non-network) client printers only**: This setting will only allow the auto-creation of locally attached client printers. This setting will prohibit network printers from being auto-created from client device.

- **Do not auto-create client printers**: This setting will disallow any client printers from being auto-created in ICA session.

Auto-create generic universal printer

The Auto-create generic universal printer policy controls the Citrix Universal Printer feature. The Citrix Universal Printer is disabled by default on XenApp 6.0 or XenDesktop 5.0 and the higher versions. You need to enable it under this policy to make use of the Citrix Universal Printer and UPD driver.

Client printer names

The Client printer names policy controls the naming convention to be used in XenApp or XenDesktop printer mapping. By default, standard printer names similar to Terminal Service are used; for example, *HPLaserJet 1 from client name in session 2*.

You can select **Legacy printer names** under this policy to enable backward compatibility for the old Metaframe-style printers that have the naming convention as *Client/Clientname#/HPLaserJet1*.

Direct connections to print servers

The Direct connections to print servers policy enables or disables the direct connections that are to be used for host to network printer connections. By default, the direct connections are enabled.

For fast communication in a LAN environment, it is always recommended to enable direct connections.

Printer mapping and driver compatibility

With the Printer mapping and driver compatibility policy, you can create rules to control the printer mappings for a specific driver. You can also use the driver compatibility feature to auto-create client printers using Citrix Universal Print driver only. You can also choose or provide a replacement driver for conflicting drivers by creating a specific rule under this policy:

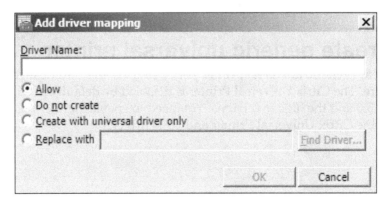

Printer properties retention

The Printer properties retention policy is used to define where to store the printer properties. By default, the printer properties are stored on either the client device or user profile. There are four different ways to control the printer properties using this policy:

- **Held in profile if not saved on client**: This setting will force the system to store printer properties on a client device if possible. If the printer properties are not stored on a client machine, it will save the properties on the user profile.

- **Retained in user profile only**: This setting will force systems to store the printer properties in the user profile only.

- **Saved on client device only**: This setting will force the system to store the printer properties on a client device only.

- **Do not retain printer properties**: This will prohibit you from saving the printer properties.

Retain and restore client printers

The Retain and restore client printers policy lets you choose if you want to retain and restore a client's auto-created printers or not. By default, this policy is enabled to retain the client's auto-created printers and restore them in the next session launched by the user.

You can disable this feature by selecting the **Prohibit** option under this policy.

Automatic installation of in-box drivers

The Automatic installation of in-box drivers policy provides a control to enable or disable the automatic installation of in-box printer drivers and is enabled by default.

You can restrict the automatic installation of in-box drivers by choosing the **Disabled** option under this policy.

Universal driver preference

The Universal driver preference policy allows you to control UPD driver preferences; you can add, remove, and alter the driver preference order as per your requirements:

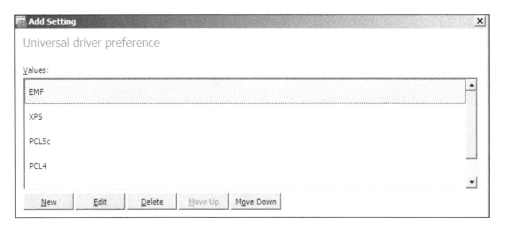

 For details on each of the preference formats in the preceding screenshot, you can refer to the *Printing* section in *XenDesktop Handbook 7.x* available at http://support.citrix.com/content/dam/supportWS/kA460000000CoLKCA0/Citrix_Virtual_Desktop_Handbook_%287x%29.pdf.

Universal Print Driver usage

The Universal Print Driver usage policy is used to configure Citrix UPD usage. You can configure the policy settings to specify when to use universal printing and when to force the use of the generic Universal Print Driver instead of the printer model-specific native drivers. The policy provides the following options to configure UPD usage:

- **Use universal printing only if the requested driver is unavailable**: This setting allows the system to make use of universal printing when no standard printer drivers are available.

- **Use only printer model-specific drivers**: This policy will ensure that no printer is auto-created using Citrix Universal Print Driver. If the standard model-specific driver is unavailable, the printer will not be created.

- **Use universal printing only**: This setting will force the system to use universal printing only. It will make use of the Universal Print Driver to create client printers.

- **Use printer model-specific driver only if universal printing is unavailable**: This setting will allow the printers to be created using a model-specific print driver if Universal Print Driver is unavailable.

Universal printing EMF processing mode

The Universal printing EMF processing mode policy controls the way in which the EMF spool files are processed from printer to the client machine. By default, all EMF spool files are directly sent to the client's Windows subsystem to be processed. However, there are some printers where the EMF format might not be compatible; in that case the EMF spool files are reprocessed under the GDI subsystem, before being sent to the client for processing.

 If you are unaware if your printers support the EMF format for printing, it is recommended to force the **Re-process EMFs for printer** setting under this policy.

Universal printing image compression limit

The Universal printing image compression limit policy defines the maximum quality and minimum compression level for the images printed using Universal Print Driver. By default, the best quality is selected for lossless compression. You can alter the settings under this policy for image quality and compression.

Universal printer optimization defaults

The Universal printer optimization defaults policy provides the default settings for the universal printer created during the ICA session. This setting provides the following options to control the optimization behavior:

- Desired image quality

- Enable heavyweight compression

- Allow caching of embedded images

- Allow caching of embedded fonts

- Allow non-administrators to modify these settings

By default, standard image quality is selected. However, you can alter these settings to get the desired image quality. Please refer to the following screenshot for the policy outlook:

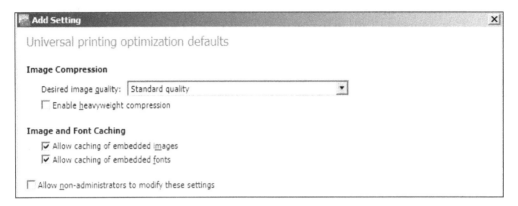

 This policy requires the printing optimization pack to be installed on XenApp 6.0 or later. This doesn't apply to XenDesktop.

Universal printing preview preference

The Universal printing preview preference policy defines whether to use the print preview function for auto-created or generic universal printers. By default, this policy disables the print preview function.

You can alter the settings under this policy to make use of the print preview function for auto-created printers, generic universal printers, or both:

- **Universal printing print quality limit**: It specifies the maximum DPI (dots per inch) available for generating the print output in the ICA session.

- **Wait for printers to be created**: This policy controls whether you want the printers to be created while the desktop is launched or not. This should be disabled as we don't want the printers to delay the desktop launch.

Exploring the XenDesktop® printing registry settings

XenDesktop uses a different way to implement the `DefaultPrnFlags` registry setting. Unlike XenApp, where multiple sessions run on the server at the same time, VDAs in XenDesktop run only a single sessions at a time.

So, it doesn't store a farm-wide configuration in the `DefaultPrnFlags` key in each VDA agent. XenDesktop employs a different approach of using XML blob where both farm and policy wide information is passed to each Virtual Desktop Agent during the start of a session. The information is captured at the desktop Delivery Controller from various resources and then passed in the form of an XML document.

You can use the **PortICASetDefaults** tool to set the DefaultSessionFlags value in XenDesktop. When a logon is initiated, session settings for printing are collected from policies, Terminal Services defaults, and the DefaultSessionFlags value from the XML blob.

You can modify the system default values by the following procedure:

1. Log in to the Delivery Controller server and browse to the following directory: `C:\Program Files\Citrix\Desktop Delivery Controller\`.

2. Run the following command on a CMD prompt to extract the Default XML Blob:

   `PortICASetDefaults /o <Directory>\<FileName.txt>`

3. Open the extracted file with Notepad and look for the opening `<session>` tag. Now, paste the following immediately after the `<session>` tag:

   ```
   <PrinterManagement><DefaultSessionFlags>value</
   DefaultSessionFlags></PrinterManagement>
   ```

This value is calculated by adding together the decimal values decided upon from the table provided by Citrix, as given at http://support.citrix.com/servlet/KbServlet/download/18846-102-722088/CTXPRN_OVERRIDE_TS_DEFAULTS.pdf.

Make sure that you add 128 to the value to override the Terminal Services defaults if the setting you want is marked as having a Terminal Services default value.

4. Save the file and run the following command:

```
PortICASetDefaults /i <Directory>\<FileName.txt>
```

5. To revert the values to the default, use the following command:

```
PortICASetDefaults /d
```

Using Print Detective and StressPrinters

Troubleshooting printing problems can become a headache if we are not using the right set of tools needed to diagnose the problem. Citrix has developed the Print Detective and StressPrinters tools to diagnose and resolve these issues.

 Citrix recommends using Citrix universal printing and if the print policies and Citrix universal printing are configured optimally, you won't have any major issues in your XenDesktop environment.

We have explained the basic setup and usage of these tools in *Chapter 2, Troubleshooting Toolkit for Citrix XenDesktop®*, to troubleshoot common Citrix printing problems that surface in a Citrix XenDesktop environment. To learn more about using these tools, please refer *Chapter 2, Troubleshooting Toolkit for Citrix XenDesktop®*.

Summary

We should now have a good understanding of the XenDesktop printing setup, print policies and the tools required to troubleshoot major printing issues that might arise in a XenDesktop environment.

In our next chapter, we will focus on configuring and setting up the right set of HDX MediaStream policies required for a XenDesktop environment to provide the smoothest and best visual experience to the endusers.

Getting the Better of HDX™ MediaStream Challenges

9

In the last chapter, we discussed the printing architecture and solved the common printing issues that you may encounter while working in a Citrix XenDesktop environment.

We will now focus on Citrix XenDesktop HDX policies and their configuration, which is a key area to optimizing the performance in any XenDesktop deployment. If the policies and rules are not set in the right direction, the administrators might end up with a XenDesktop deployment that is totally unstable and the users will complain every now and then about performance issues.

In this chapter, we will cover the following points:

- Understanding the HDX display modes
- HDX policies and their impact on user experience
- Using Flash Redirection for a smooth HDX experience
- Working with HDX RealTime audio/video and the HDX plugin for Microsoft Lync 2010

Understanding the HDX™ display modes

Citrix HDX was introduced in February 2009 with Citrix XenDesktop 3.0 and since then, many features have been added and improvements have been made to this technology to deliver the best possible user experience.

There are basically three main delivery methods that need to be taken care of while configuring HDX policies in your XenApp or XenDesktop environment. They are as follows:

- Desktop Composition Redirection or DCR
- H.264-enhanced SuperCodec
- Legacy graphics mode

Desktop Composition Redirection

Desktop Composition Redirection can be enabled only for desktop OS VDAs in a XenDesktop environment. DCR operates at the level of Windows Desktop Manager, which means that we can now manage the Windows UI using GPU at the end user device, leveraging the DirectX feature of Windows endpoints.

It supports Mac OS X 10.7, 10.8, 10.9, and 10.10 as well as Windows 7, Windows 8, and also the latest Windows OS.

H.264-enhanced SuperCodec

H.264 is the HDX SuperCodec. It's a collection of codecs that is optimized for handing different types of data. The codec is encoded with the new encoder to optimize Windows drawing in Windows 8's and Windows 2012's new display architecture.

 To read more on GDI that controls the graphics in Windows, please read MSDN article at `https://msdn.microsoft.com/en-us/library/aa925824.aspx`.

The Citrix Legacy display driver, which was being used till now, is based on the GDI commands to support the Windows display driver. However, with the introduction of Windows 8 it has become obsolete. So, Citrix has to come up with an improved and better SuperCodec using the adaptive H.264 technology.

If any enduser device is running a non-H.264 based receiver, the user would still be able to work using the fallback compatibility. Citrix doesn't recommend using this until and unless there is a real dependency of other legacy apps that can't work using the new receiver.

The legacy graphics mode

The legacy graphics mode was the display mode that was used in the earlier XenApp and XenDesktop versions. Lots of improvements have been made in this mode, such as Progressive Display, extra color compression, and lastly Adaptive Display, to deliver the operating system graphics using Microsoft GDI.

Refer to the following table for the display modes versus operating system matrix that will give you a fair idea about which display modes are supported by various operating systems:

Operating system	DCR	H.264 SuperCodec supported	H.264 fallback mode	Legacy graphics mode
Windows 8	Yes	Yes[ab]	Yes	NA
Windows 7 Aero	Yes	Yes[ab]	Yes	Yes[a]
Windows 7	NA	Yes[ab]	Yes	Yes
Windows Vista Aero	Yes	NA (limitation due to legacy VDA agent)	NA (limitation due to legacy VDA agent)	Yes[a]
Windows Vista	NA	NA (limitation due to legacy VDA agent)	NA (limitation due to legacy VDA agent)	Yes
Windows XP	NA	NA (limitation due to legacy VDA agent)	NA	Yes
Windows 2012 R2	NA	Yes[ab]	Yes, but not recommended	Yes
Windows 2008 R2	NA	Yes[ab]	Yes	Yes

(ᵃ): Even if the legacy graphics mode is enabled by a policy for a VDA agent, DCR can still be used to provide the Aero experience to the users unless:

- DCR has been disabled by a policy
- The endpoint client is DCR-capable
- The Aero theme has been applied for the session

(ᵃᵇ): H.264 requires the following receiver versions:

Operating system	Receiver version
Windows	3.4 and above
Mac OS	11.8 and later
Android	3.5
iOS	5.9
Chrome OS	1.4

HDX™ policies and their impact on user experience

There is a long list of Citrix HDX graphics policies; sometimes it becomes very difficult to understand which one should be configured to provide an optimal user experience.

So, we will be going through all the relevant and important HDX policies that every administrator must be aware of to configure.

Desktop Composition graphics quality

The Desktop Composition graphics quality policy helps us define the quality of graphics for Desktop Composition Redirection.

There are four settings that can be used to set the graphics quality; **High**, **Medium**, **Low**, or **Lossless**, as shown in the following screenshot:

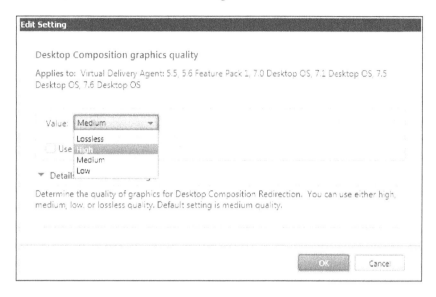

Desktop Composition Redirection

The Desktop Composition Redirection policy allows us to redirect the desktop composition from VDA to the endpoint device to provide an enriched user experience.

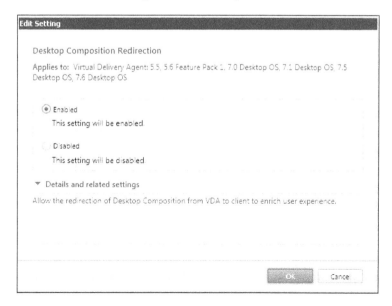

The Desktop Composition feature was introduced with Windows Vista and it actually changed the way applications display pixels to form an image on the screen. With the desktop composition enabled, all the windows drawings happen off-screen in the video memory, which is then rendered to the desktop image and it forms a display.

Enhanced Desktop Experience

The Enhanced Desktop Experience policy helps us to configure the server OSs to deliver the closest desktop OS look possible. This is useful when you are publishing XenApp desktops or hosted shared desktops:

Please make a note that this policy won't be applied for the users who already have their profiles created on the server. As a result, you will need to reset the user profile. Also, ensure that you don't share roaming profiles between server and desktop OSs.

Display memory limit

The Display memory limit policy allows us to set the maximum video buffer size for the session in Kbytes; the default value is set to 65,536 KB. If you use color depth and higher resolution, you will have to increase this value as it requires more memory. The range is between 128–131,072. Upon reaching the memory threshold, the session display is degraded to the **Display mode degrade preference** setting:

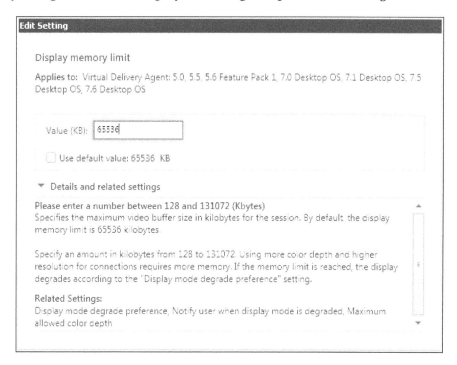

 The **Display Mode Degrade Preference** option is only available when we use the legacy graphics mode. This is not applicable when we are using the latest DCR or H.264 SuperCodec graphics.

Dynamic windows preview

The Dynamic windows preview policy enables the seamless Windows preview to be seen on the published applications; this is applicable just for XenApp and is enabled by default.

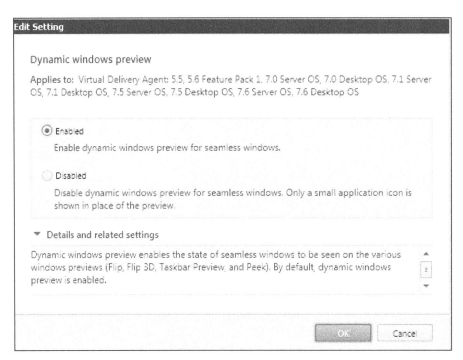

Image caching

As the name suggests, the Image caching policy is used to cache images to make the scrolling smoother. This works only in the legacy graphics mode.

Legacy graphics mode

The legacy graphics mode policy can be used to turn on the legacy graphics mode for the end users using legacy Citrix clients, as shown in the following screenshot:

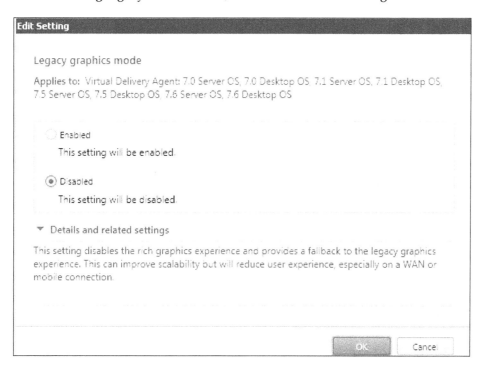

Maximum allowed color depth

The Maximum allowed color depth policy is enabled while using the legacy graphics mode and specifies the maximum allowed color depth for a session. By default, it is set to 32 bits per pixel as shown in the following screenshot. Setting this value higher means that you require more memory per session.

You need to consider the **Display Memory Limit** and **Display mode degrade preference** settings accordingly.

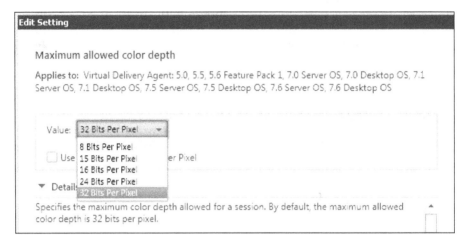

Notify user when display mode is degraded

The Notify user when experience is degraded policy is disabled by default and the experience is degraded silently for a user. This is applicable only while using RDS. When this policy is enabled, it displays a pop-up when the color depth or resolution is degraded as per the **Display mode degrade preference** setting, as shown in the following screenshot:

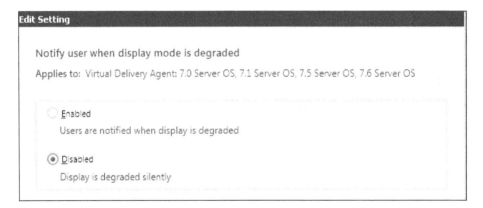

Persistent cache threshold

The Persistent cache threshold policy allows us to control the caching threshold of bitmap images on the client machines. This enables us to re-use the large cached images from the previous user sessions. You can even adjust the bandwidth threshold value in Kbps below which will enable the persistent cache. The default value is set to 3,000,000 Kbps.

This policy is applicable only while using the legacy graphics mode.

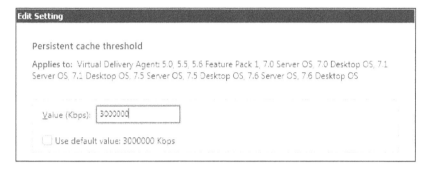

Queuing and tossing

The Queuing and tossing policy is used to discard queued images, which have been replaced by another image. Ensure that you disable this policy if you need to run animations. This is applicable only with the legacy graphics mode. It is shown in the following screenshot.

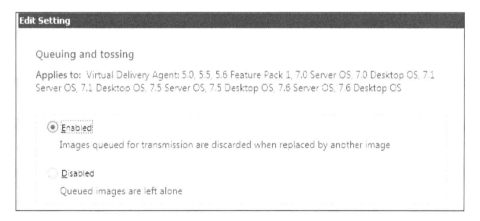

Extra color compression

The Extra color compression policy allows us to manage the color compression for images. By enabling this setting, you can improve the responsiveness of low bandwidth connections. However, it can impact the quality of images displayed to the users.

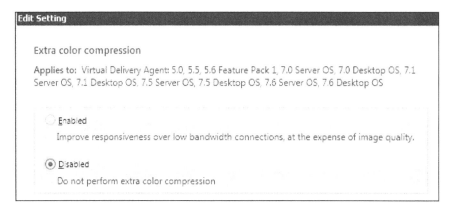

Extra color compression threshold

The Extra color compression threshold policy allows us to control the threshold at which the color compression is applied. The default value is 8,192 Kbps. You can set any value between 0 and 4,294,967. This setting is applicable only while using the legacy graphics mode:

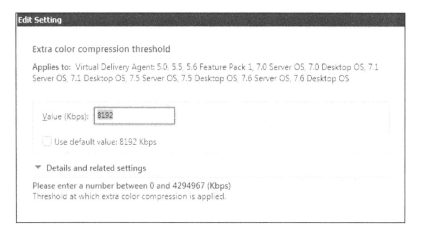

Heavyweight compression

The Heavyweight compression policy helps us to reduce the bandwidth consumption without losing much of the image quality using an advanced CPU-intensive graphic algorithm. This compression is disabled by default and is only used with Citrix Receiver and has no effect while using other legacy Citrix ICA clients.

This setting is only applicable when using the legacy graphics mode:

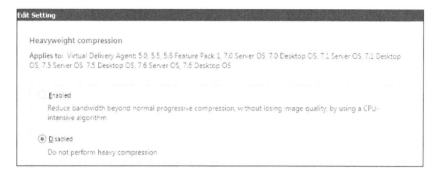

Lossy compression level

The Lossy compression level policy is one of the compression policies used to save bandwidth to improve session responsiveness. This is generally avoided if image quality and data is vital for a customer. An example of such a case is while processing X-ray images or using AutoCAD 3D modeling.

If enabled, the policy uses the Lossy compression threshold value setting while processing the images for compression. The default value is set to **Medium** for this policy.

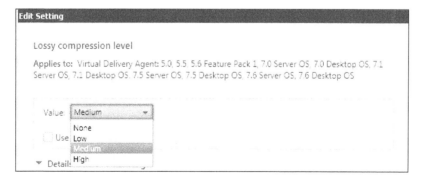

Lossy compression threshold value

The Lossy compression threshold value policy controls the bandwidth requirement of sessions where you want to enable the lossy compression. By default, this is set to unlimited, which means the session will be enabled to go through the lossy compression. You should set the threshold value as per the requirement between 0 and 2,147,483,647 Kbps.

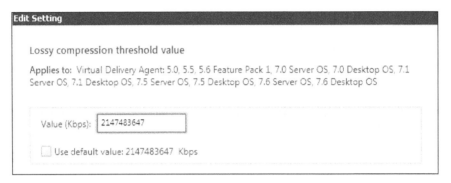

Minimum image quality

The Minimum image quality policy controls the Adaptive Display minimum acceptable image quality for moving images while using the legacy graphics mode. The default value is **Normal** and you can set the value anywhere between **Low** (lowest quality) and **Ultra High** (highest quality) settings, as shown in the following screenshot:

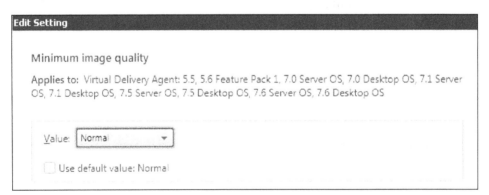

Moving image compression

The Moving image compression policy enables or disables the Adaptive Display when using the legacy graphics mode; the Adaptive and Progressive Display cannot work simultaneously. When one is enabled, the other gets disabled automatically.

 Progressive Display is a legacy feature which is not recommended to be enabled at anytime in your XenDesktop deployment.

This policy is always enabled by default. If you want to disable the Adaptive Display, you can disable this policy, as shown here:

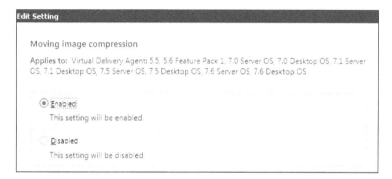

Progressive compression level

With the Progressive compression level policy, you can provide a faster initial display for the images compared to lossy compression. However, for progressive compression to be effective in your deployment, always ensure that its values are set higher than the lossy compression values. By default, progressive compression level settings are not set.

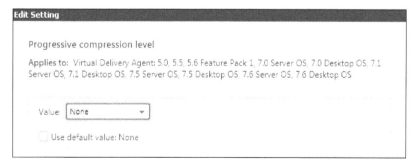

Progressive compression threshold value

The Progressive compression threshold value policy is used to define the bandwidth under which compression would be applied on the sessions. You can set the value between 0 and 214,748,364 Kbps. By default, the value is unlimited:

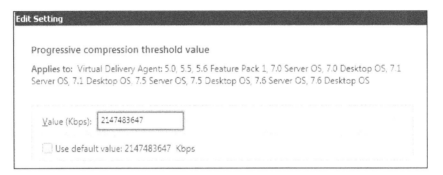

Target frame rate

The Target frame rate policy provides you with an option to configure the maximum number of frames per second that the virtual desktop will send to the client. The maximum and default setting is 30 fps, as shown in the following screenshot. You shouldn't change this setting unless you want to reduce the bandwidth and resource consumption at the expense of user experience.

This setting is applicable while using any of the graphics mode, be it DCR, H.264 SuperCodec, or the legacy graphics mode.

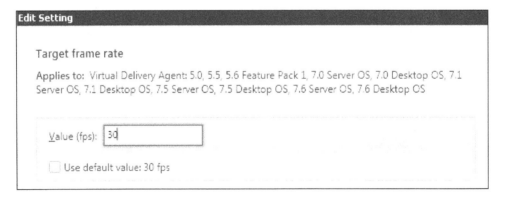

Target minimum frame rate

The Target minimum frame rate policy provides a control to maintain a minimum target frame rate in a low bandwidth session. This is applicable for legacy Adaptive Display only, as shown here:

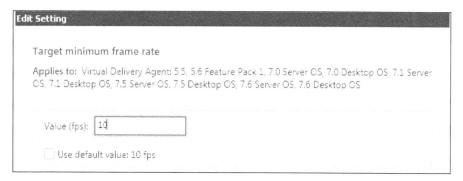

Visual quality

The Visual quality policy allows you to control the visual quality of the images. The higher the visual quality, the higher will be the bandwidth requirement of the users. The default setting is for medium visual quality, as shown in the following screenshot.

It can be configured in five visual quality modes: **Low**, **Medium**, **High**, **Build to Lossless**, and **Always Lossless**. When the data is playing a vital role and you don't want to compromise on the visual quality of images, select the **Always Lossless** option.

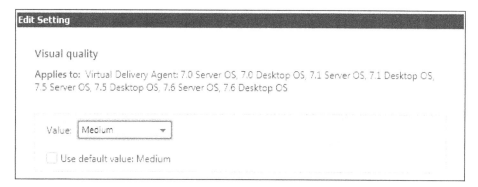

Using Flash Redirection for a smooth HDX™ experience

To provide the users with an uninterrupted and flawless video experience, we should always configure Flash Redirection that will force the Flash processing to happen on the user device. To configure Flash Redirection, we require two types of Flash players:

- Adobe Flash Player for Internet Explorer

- Adobe Flash Player for other browsers; for example, **Netscape Plugin Application Programming Interface (NPAPI)**

 To know about the systems supported for Flash Redirection and all the prerequisites, refer the Citrix article at `https://www.citrix.com/support/product-lifecycle/product-matrix`.

Citrix recommends you to configure Flash Redirection with client-side rendering and client-side fetching wherever possible. This will always provide a better user experience by utilizing local device resources to display the Flash content.

When configuring a second-generation Flash Redirection, you should take the following considerations into account to ensure an optimal experience that has to be provided to the users:

- Flash Redirection is enabled by default via the **Flash default behavior** policy of Citrix XenDesktop 7.x. There are other additional policies that are provided to control this behavior in a much better way, such as **Flash intelligent fallback** and whitelist and blacklist options.

- The Flash intelligent fallback option automatically reverts to the server side rendering wherever client-side rendering doesn't work or provides a poor user experience.

- Ensure that the clients are using Citrix Receiver v3.4 and above and have enough system resources.

- Validate with Adobe before committing or implementing any solution based on the GPU based processing.

- Flash Redirection is supported on Linux and Windows operating systems.

- Citrix Consulting recommends to implement client-side rendering and client-side fetching wherever possible. However, there is one important thing to note here: when a client fetches multimedia content from the Internet, it utilizes the same connection it uses for HDX traffic. So, you might face network contention if QoS is not implemented in your deployment.

- For optimum experience, Citrix recommends to implement 2 vCPUs on each desktop VM for best Flash Redirection performance.

- If you have a heavy Flash Redirection load, Citrix recommends to leverage Citrix Branch Repeater as a WAN optimization solution.

To troubleshoot issues related to HDX redirection, your go-to tool will be HDX Monitor. We have already gone through the tool configurations and troubleshooting methodology in *Chapter 2, Troubleshooting Toolkit for Citrix XenDesktop®*.

Working with HDX™ RealTime audio/video and the HDX™ plugin for Microsoft Lync 2010

Many customers look for audio/video conferencing that can be achieved easily via remote means. They need not be present in offices all the time to attend meetings and Citrix HDX RealTime is a technology that enables users working on Citrix apps and virtual desktops to join audio/video conferencing smoothly.

The key features of HDX RealTime are as follows:

- **TCP audio jitter buffer**: This is a Citrix Receiver audio enhancement feature which utilizes buffering to counter attack and improve the performance of the packet switched networks that bring audio jitter along with them. With this enhancement, end users receive a smooth playback of audio and videos on a virtual desktop. The buffering of jitter brings in some latency but that is taken care of by XenDesktop latency reduction audio stack.

- **UDP for audio**: Another feature that HDX RealTime brings to you is the ability to utilize UDP for audio in a multimedia conference. By taking advantage of using UDP as a protocol for sending and receiving audio, it avoids the lag that can occur with TCP when there is a network congestion or packet loss. This is best suited for voice over telephony and can be set under XenDesktop policies.

- **Microphone redirection**: This feature enables the audio device redirection to happen over Citrix Receiver to utilize the end user's local audio input. You can set this option using XenDesktop audio policies.

 In Citrix validation testing, UDP outperformed TCP in audio quality. Citrix Consulting recommends using the UDP for audio feature if you have users separated geographically on WAN connections and using VOIP applications for audio/video conferencing.

The key points to note are as follows:

- UDP for audio uses no more bandwidth than the TCP protocol while delivering superior audio quality.
- If you want to do video conferencing, make sure that you enable the Windows Media Redirection policy.
- If using softphone or other VOIP apps, please configure the audio quality policy to be modified to have them medium-optimized for a speed setting to reduce any excessive data transfer overhead.

Many organizations have been using Microsoft Lync as a strategic application to do video/audio conferencing. Citrix took this as an opportunity to step up and develop a HDX RealTime optimization pack for Microsoft Lync 2010 in June 2012. With the release of XenDesktop 7.6 FP1, Citrix has released v1.7 for the HDX RealTime optimization pack for Lync 2013 clients on Windows and Linux platforms.

The HDX RealTime optimization pack is built upon an optimized architecture that offloads media processing onto the user device maximizing server scalability and improvising audio/video quality delivered to the end users.

 HDX RealTime v1.7 is a part of XenApp and XenDesktop 7.6 FP1; it is still fully compatible to work with XenApp 6.x and XenDesktop 5.x product suites.

Citrix fully supports the Microsoft VDI plugin for Lync 2013 but sometimes it becomes difficult for customers to decide which plugin they should go with. You should take a note of the following points that clearly explain why we need the HDX optimization pack for Lync:

- The Microsoft VDI plugin for Lync supports only Windows devices, whereas the Citrix HDX optimization pack supports Windows, Linux, and Mac devices.

- The HDX optimization pack gives you an option to publish Lync as the published application.

- The HDX optimization pack supports Lync Online / Office365.

- The Microsoft VDI plugin just supports Lync 2013 whereas the HDX optimization pack supports Lync 2010 as well as Lync 2013.

- The HDX optimization pack falls back to ICA MediaStream if no MediaStream engine is found on the user device.

To configure the HDX optimization pack for Lync 2013, you need to download the latest pack from the Citrix Downloads section. Once downloaded, it will contain two components:

- **The client component**: This includes the Citrix HDX RealTime MediaStream engine that integrates with the Citrix Receiver on the enduser device and is responsible for doing all the processing at the client device.

- **The server component**: This includes the Citrix HDX RealTime Connector for Microsoft Lync that interacts with the Lync client which in turn utilizes the client MediaStream engine to start processing at the client device.

There are some limitations to this new version; some of the important ones are as follows:

- No support for Lync Basic for RealTime connector, you need to use the full version of Lync

- No support for response groups

- Delegation not supported

- No access to voicemail and playback

- No recording

- The auto-discovery to locate Lync servers still needs to use the DNS/SRV method for Lync server discovery

- No **Call** and **Video Call** buttons in the Lync contact card

- Issues with multimedia redirection in Linux devices

The HDX optimization pack v1.7 seems promising to serve the enterprise customer needs. But, it still has not been tested and proven. So, make sure that you analyze all the options and choose what's best for your customers.

Summary

We now have a good understanding of the Citrix HDX display modes and important HDX policies required to be configured to provide optimal visual experience to end users in a virtual desktop environment.

In our next chapter, we will focus on working with Citrix PVS and MCS challenges and issues we might face in configuring both the environments for our virtual desktop deployments.

10
Taming MCS and PVS™ Setbacks Gracefully

In the last chapter, we discussed Citrix HDX display modes and important HDX policies that need to be configured to provide an optimal visual experience to endusers on a virtual desktop environment.

We will now focus on troubleshooting common **Machine Creation Services** (**MCS**) and **Provisioning Services** (**PVS**) configuration issues that may arise in your Citrix XenDesktop environment during daily operations.

In this chapter, we will cover the following points:

- Enabling logging for MCS and PVS
- Using MCS service logging to troubleshoot common issues
- Troubleshooting the PVS stream service and console issues
- Overcoming common PVS issues

Enabling logging for MCS and PVS™

To troubleshoot any environment, you must have proper logging enabled to provide you with an insight about what caused the issue. So, we will now look at the options that we have to configure the right set of logging features for both MCS and PVS services.

You can download the LogEnabler utility to enable the right set of logging required on the controller and VDA for all the required services of MCS.

To download and configure the LogEnabler utility for your environment, visit http://support.citrix.com/article/CTX127492.

To collect PVS logs, Citrix has developed a tool called PVSDataTools and this can be downloaded and configured easily to collect diagnostic information by following the instructions provided with the tool. Later, the traces collected by this tool are uploaded to the Citrix Insight Services website or to https://taas.citrix.com to get the analysis done. You can also use any third-party log parser utility to do the analysis yourself.

 You can download and configure the latest version of PVSDataTools by visiting http://support.citrix.com/article/CTX136079.

There are other ways as well to enable logging using PowerShell commands, CDF trace, and Citrix Scout; these have been explained earlier in *Chapter 2, Troubleshooting Toolkit for Citrix XenDesktop®*, which you can refer to for more details.

You also have a default logging level that can be enabled on the provisioning server and target device on the PVS console by following these steps:

1. Log in to the Citrix PVS server and open the PVS Console MMC snap-in.
2. Go to **Servers** | **server** | **Properties** | **Logging**. For the **Logging level** option, select **Trace** for verbose logging, as shown in the following screenshot:

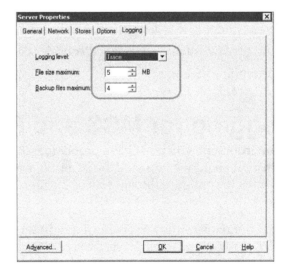

If you select the **Log events to the server's Windows Event Log** option, as shown in the following screenshot, all events will be logged to Windows Event Viewer instead of the default path `C:\ProgramData\Citrix\Provisioning Services\Log`.

There are seven logging levels that you can select, the **Trace** option will give you the most verbose results:

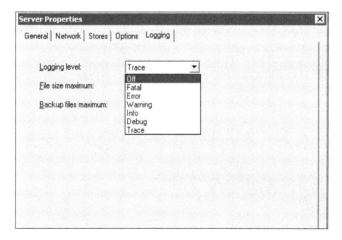

3. To configure target device logging, open the Provisioning Services Console. Go to **Device Collections** | **Collection** | **target device** | **Properties** | **Logging**. Set the **Logging level** option to **Trace**:

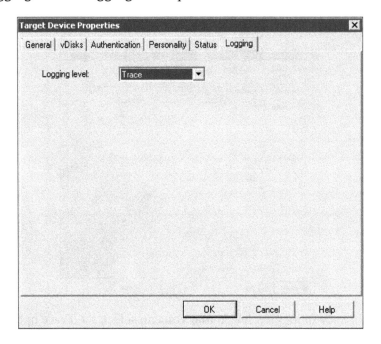

The target device logging should be set at the same level as, or lower than, the logging level that is set at the server level. If the client level logging is set to **Trace** and server level logging is set to **Error**, then the client will only log errors. Target device logs are also logged to Citrix Provisioning Server logs; you can view the events viewer on the Citrix PVS server and check PVS logs under the default path on the Citrix PVS server.

The data collected by these logs will help you to troubleshoot issues related to MCS, PVS, and other broker communication issues. These logs are a must for deep level analysis and troubleshooting and even Citrix Support requires these logs to be uploaded once you open a new case with them.

Using MCS service logging for troubleshooting common issues

Once the XenDesktop service logging is enabled for all relevant MCS-related services, we are ready to collect logs and troubleshoot any issue that arises in a XenDesktop environment due to misconfiguration or communication problems with these components.

Before proceeding to look at the service logs, we just want to highlight that there are some common areas that can be a cause of issues pertaining to MCS:

- Hypervisor communication
- Domain permissions
- Failed database entries
- Host-to-storage connection issues
- Naming convention issues with host

Let's look at a case study to understand MCS issues while creating a catalog and adding machines.

Case study – Machine Creation Services fail while creating a catalog

This may happen if you have recently migrated your XenDesktop 5.x environment to a XenDesktop 7.x site and have not adjusted the vCenter permissions required for the XenDesktop 7.x site.

Let's look at the error you receive while creating a new catalog for MCS.

The following screenshot shows the error details:

```
New-Item : The user does not have appropriate permission at the hypervisor (Either the account is not granted
sufficient privilege or disabled or username/password is incorrect)
        + CategoryInfo : InvalidOperation: (:) [New-Item], InvalidOperationException
        + FullyQualifiedErrorId :
Citrix.XDPowerShell.HostStatus.HypervisorPermissionDenied,Microsoft.PowerShell.Commands.NewItemCommand
    New-Item : The user does not have appropriate permission at the hypervisor (Either the account is not granted
sufficient privilege or disabled or username/password is incorrect)
        + CategoryInfo : NotSpecified: (:) [New-Item], InvalidOperationException
        + FullyQualifiedErrorId :
System.InvalidOperationException,Microsoft.PowerShell.Commands.NewItemCommand


Inner Exception:
    System.InvalidOperationException The user does not have appropriate permission at the hypervisor (Either the
account is not granted sufficient privilege or disabled or username/password is incorrect)
```

This happens because the new XenDesktop 7.x site admin doesn't have the required permissions on the vCenter resources. XenDesktop 7.x and higher versions require the site admin account to have two or more vCenter permissions:

- **VirtualMachine.Config.AdvancedConfig**: This is accessible from **Virtual machine | Configuration | Advanced**

- **VirtualMachine.Config.Settings**: This is accessible from **Virtual machine | Configuration | Settings**

 For more details on vCenter service account permissions, visit http://docs.citrix.com/en-us/xenapp-and-xendesktop/7-1/cds-integrate-wrapper-rho/cds-vmware-rho.html.

Once permissions are fixed, you will be able to create MCS catalogs.

For additional details on the errors, you can always refer to the **Logging** tab in Citrix Studio and the MCS log that you have configured to save the logs at the c:\XDLogs\MCS.log path or any other relevant location on your broker.

The following screenshot shows the MCS log:

```
                                 MCS - Notepad                                  _  □  x
 File  Edit  Format  View  Help
 19/07/15 19:05:32.4692 : MachineCreationIsm:WcfClientBase.RegisteredCallAndRetry CurrentServiceInstance:
 19/07/15 19:05:32.4692 : MachineCreationIsm:Enter:WcfClientBase.SelectNewConnection
 19/07/15 19:05:32.4692 : MachineCreationIsm:Enter:InterServiceManager.GetPreferredServiceInstance
 serviceFamily:serviceTypeName:'Admin' interfaceType:'InterService' minVersion:1 maxVersion:1
 19/07/15 19:05:32.4692 : MachineCreationIsm:InterServiceManager.PopulateCacheIfRequired enter
 19/07/15 19:05:32.4692 : MachineCreationIsm:InterServiceManager.PopulateCacheIfRequired lock acquired
 19/07/15 19:05:32.4692 : MachineCreationIsm:InterServiceManager.PopulateCacheIfRequired exit
 19/07/15 19:05:32.4692 : MachineCreationIsm:InterServiceManager.GetPreferredServiceInstance |
 preferredServiceInstance:ServiceGroupName:'Citrix_XD' ServiceGroupUid:22541cc9-4319-4493-a0b1-7965baf5cb23
 ServiceInstanceUid:ab2c7057-7be6-4ba6-9c8b-14c5f893164d
 Address:'http://citrix01.testlab.com/Citrix/DelegatedAdminContract/DelegatedAdminAPI/v1' Binding:wcf_HTTP_kerb Version:1
 ServiceAccount:'TESTLAB\XD-001$' ServiceAccountSid:S-1-5-21-962264046-888720465-393826521-76512
 InterfaceType:InterService FailureTime: 01/01/0001 00:00:00
 19/07/15 19:05:32.4692 : MachineCreationIsm:WcfClientBase.SelectNewConnection: CurrentServiceInstance:
 ServiceGroupName:'Citrix_XD' ServiceGroupUid:22541cc9-4319-4493-a0b1-7965baf5cb23 ServiceInstanceUid:ab2c7057-7be6-4ba6
 -9c8b-14c5f893164d Address:'http://citrix01.testlab.com/Citrix/DelegatedAdminContract/DelegatedAdminAPI/v1'
 Binding:wcf_HTTP_kerb Version:1 ServiceAccount:'TESTLAB\XD-001$' ServiceAccountSid:S-1-5-21-962264046-888720465-
 393826521-76512 InterfaceType:InterService FailureTime: 01/01/0001 00:00:00
 19/07/15 19:05:32.4692 : MachineCreationIsm:Enter:WcfClientBase.CallAndRetryInternal T:
 Citrix.InterService.DelegatedAdminApi.IDelegatedAdminApi, TResult:System.Boolean
```

There can be multiple MCS-related issues that will come your way while creating catalogs, managing host connections, adding new brokers, and so on. The basics remain the same: you need to configure logging for the required services and then you are ready to dig down to troubleshoot.

Troubleshooting PVS™ Streaming Service and console issues

Citrix PVS is a technology that provides us with an alternate procedure to clone and deploy large number of machines efficiently. This technology allows us to create clones for both XenDesktop and XenApp.

We must remember that a PVS Streaming Server or PVS server provides a PXE bootstrap and holds all the records of the target systems via bound MAC addresses in its database. When a target requests a vDisk, the MAC address is checked in the PVS database and the relevant vDisk is provided for the device to boot off of using a TFTP service on the PVS server.

Now the key points to note here are:

- PVS depends upon a network boot using PXE (there can be an exception to it when using a boot device manager to boot vDisks)
- Write cache location required for each target device
- A PVS store where all the vDisks are kept
- A hypervisor layer where all VMs reside

The preceding points are checkpoints before you begin troubleshooting PVS-related issues. You must review your settings on a PVS console.

The Citrix PVS Streaming Service is a critical component of the Citrix PVS environment. Any issue with the stream process or service will break down streaming from the Citrix PVS streaming server. If the targets are going in to an unresponsive state too often or are having issues in booting, consider enabling stream service logs.

With PVS 7.1 and above, you can't see the stream and other PVS service logs in the `C:\ProgramData\Citrix\Provisioning Services\Log` folder. You need to run PVSDataTools to extract the logs to troubleshoot issues.

 For any issues related to the PVS console, please check the status of Citrix PVS Soap server. Recycling this service will normally resolve any common console-related problem.

Let's look at a case study to understand PVSDataTools log analysis to resolve a PVS target booting issue.

Case study – the connection to the database failed, network connection may be down

Customer environment

- XenDesktop 7.6
- Citrix PVS 6.1
- vSphere 5.5

The error was frequently seen on the PVS and was hanging stream processes on the PVS server; thus, target devices went unresponsive on a daily basis. The first place where you should start viewing the logs will be the event viewer on the PVS server.

The exact error will look similar to the following screenshot:

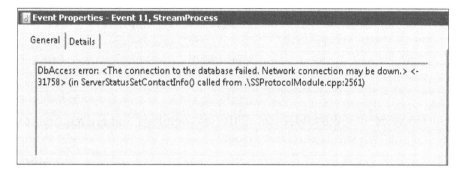

The details were provided to the database team to analyze the DB status and whether the server was having any issues or was rebooting frequently. The database team couldn't find any relevant details that could cause the issue in connectivity. Only Citrix databases were impacted and all the other application databases were working fine.

We went ahead and collected the PVS logs using PVSDataTools, to get more details on the error logs:

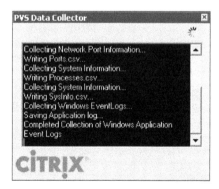

The PVSDataTools will capture all the settings of your PVS server and capture all PVS service-related logs. It will give you a ZIP folder with all the relevant details and the ZIP is created under the same path where `PVSDataCollector.exe` is placed and executed:

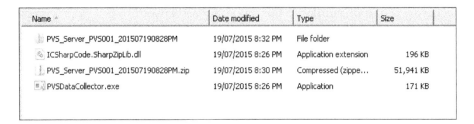

The extracted version of the folder has all the relevant logs that are required to troubleshoot any PVS services-related issue:

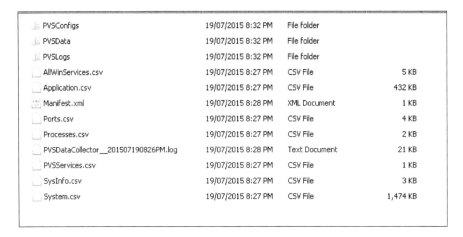

For any database connectivity issue, you need to browse to the PVS logs category and select **Stream.log**, **Streamprocess.log**, and **Console.log** to view the details for any DB connectivity issues.

Let's have a look at the following screenshot that displays the DB error that occurs while connecting with the database:

```
2015-07-19 20:23:31,615 [3] DEBUG EnterpriseAccess.MapiChannel - SPN: PVSSoap/localhost:54322
2015-07-19 20:23:31,833 [3] INFO  EnterpriseAccess.MapiChannel - Mapi channel connection timeout is 120 seconds.
2015-07-19 20:23:32,286 [3] INFO  EnterpriseAccess.Access - connected
2015-07-19 20:23:36,529 [3] INFO  EnterpriseAccess.HandlerBase - DatabaseSQLHandler
2015-07-19 20:23:36,529 [3] INFO  EnterpriseAccess.HandlerBase -   return code: 167
2015-07-19 20:23:36,529 [3] INFO  EnterpriseAccess.HandlerBase -   exception type: DatabaseSQL
2015-07-19 20:23:36,529 [3] INFO  EnterpriseAccess.HandlerBase -   message: A database SQL error occurred.
2015-07-19 20:23:36,529 [3] INFO  EnterpriseAccess.HandlerBase -   source: Mapi
2015-07-19 20:23:36,529 [3] INFO  EnterpriseAccess.HandlerBase -   inner exception type: SqlException
 015-07-19 20:23:36,529 [3] INFO  EnterpriseAccess.HandlerBase -   inner exception message: A transport-level error has
 ccurred when sending the request to the server. (provider: TCP Provider, error: 0 - An existing connection was forcibly
 losed by the remote host.)
 015-07-19 20:23:36,529 [3] INFO  EnterpriseAccess.HandlerBase -   inner exception source: .Net SqlClient Data Provider
 015-07-19 20:23:36,529 [3] INFO  EnterpriseAccess.HandlerBase -   inner exception data:
 015-07-19 20:23:36,529 [3] INFO  EnterpriseAccess.HandlerBase -     HelpLink.ProdName=Microsoft SQL Server
 015-07-19 20:23:36,529 [3] INFO  EnterpriseAccess.HandlerBase -     HelpLink.EvtSrc=MSSQLServer
 015-07-19 20:23:36,529 [3] INFO  EnterpriseAccess.HandlerBase -     HelpLink.EvtID=10054
 015-07-19 20:23:36,529 [3] INFO  EnterpriseAccess.HandlerBase -     HelpLink.BaseHelpUrl=http://go.microsoft.com/fwlink
 015-07-19 20:23:36,529 [3] INFO  EnterpriseAccess.HandlerBase -     HelpLink.LinkId=20476
 015-07-19 20:23:36,529 [3] ERROR EMCObjects.AccessEMCO - about to display exception
```

The errors in the highlighted section suggest that the connection gets forcibly closed by a remote host. We again requested the database team to look at the DB logs to check if any network interruptions are happening.

We found that the database server was having resource utilization issues that were causing our PVS server to timeout while reaching the database. The PVS database was moved to a dedicated SQL cluster for the Citrix environment to resolve this issue.

So, PVSDataTools provides you with the required details on the existing PVS configurations and error logs that can help you to diagnose issues in your XenDesktop or XenApp site.

Overcoming common PVS™ issues

There are some common Citrix PVS issues that you might face while working with a Citrix PVS environment for your XenDesktop VDI deployments.

Target devices hang at Windows startup

This issue can be due to multiple unsupported hardware on your VM; it can also be an issue with vNIC, SataController, or any other component on your Hypervisor layer. The easiest solution or workaround provided by Citrix is to enable the Interrupt Safe mode on the PVS console bootstrap configuration.

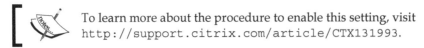

To learn more about the procedure to enable this setting, visit http://support.citrix.com/article/CTX131993.

Target devices fail to boot and display error "No entry found in Database"

This is a simple error that suggests that the device you are trying to boot doesn't have an entry in the PVS database. Sometimes, while creating PVS devices on a PVS console, administrators make a typo while entering the device MAC that matches the VM on hypervisor. You will receive this error due to the mismatch between VM and MAC address.

To resolve this error, you need to verify the MAC address on the PVS console. Once the MAC address is correctly configured, you will be able to boot your target device without any issue. There can be some scenarios where an incorrect MAC address entry caches in the PVS database and results in the error being displayed on the PXE boot screen:

```
gPXE 1.0.0 -- Open Source Boot Firmware -- http://etherboot.org
Features: AoE HTTP iSCSI DNS TFTP bzImage ELF Multiboot PXE PXEXT

net0: 72:6b:0c:77:f9:e6 on PCI00:04.0 (open)
  [Link:up, TX:0 TXE:0 RX:0 RXE:0]
DHCP (net0 72:6b:0c:77:f9:e6). ok
net0: 192.168.1.202/255.255.255.0 gw 192.168.1.1
Booting from filename "ARDBP32.BIN"
tftp://192.168.1.52/ARDBP32.BIN. ok

No entry found in database for device.

Press any key to continue...
```

To resolve such issues, you can run the following command to clear the PVS server cache:

`Executerun ForceInventory`

This command refreshes the PVS inventory. Sometimes, this doesn't resolve the issue and you can recycle these scenarios in the Citrix PVS stream services.

Target devices halt at boot screen waiting for Provisioning Services™ to respond

The error message reads *Connecting to the Provisioning Services. Please wait....* This error message is displayed on the screen suggesting that there is an issue with the PVS server. It is shown in the following screenshot:

```
CLIENT MAC ADDR: 00 50 56 98 6A D4   GUID: 4218D9CE-5BD1-FD9D-5BF5-6B91A7CCABA8
CLIENT IP: 10.28.224.151   MASK: 255.255.254.0   DHCP IP: 10.28.224.1
GATEWAY IP: 10.28.225.254

Provisioning Services bootstrap v6.1.0.1095

Copyright (c) 2001-2012 Citrix Systems, Inc. All rights reserved.

Local MAC          : 005056986AD4
Local IP           : 10.28.224.151
Subnet mask        : 255.255.254.0
Default gateway    : 10.28.225.254
Login server       : 10.28.224.1:6910
Bootstrap loaded at 9438:0000 Size 4060

Connecting to the Provisioning Services. Please wait...
```

The first troubleshooting step will be to check whether the PVS server stream service is responding successfully or not. Sometimes, PVS Streaming Service might be hung and stops responding to stream threads.

So, under event logs, just review application logs to ensure that the stream process has not got terminated unexpectedly. If you see such logs, then restarting the stream service on the PVS server will resolve this issue.

However, there can be situations where an administrator has just updated the vDisk and forgets to copy the vDisk in all the local stores on PVS servers.

You will receive this error if the vDisk is not copied to other PVS servers' local stores and vDisk load balancing is enabled. To resolve this, you need to copy the vDisk to all PVS servers' local stores and try again.

 This is valid only while using the PVS server's locally attached disk as a vDisk store. The troubleshooting step will be to change the PVS vDisk LB to serve from the primary server from where the administrator has just updated the vDisk.

Target devices give a BSOD

Sometimes, booting target devices using PXE network boot and using DHCP can land you in difficult situations where you won't be able to boot devices and you see a **blue screen of death** (**BSOD**) for multiple targets.

The blue screen of death on PVS targets can be seen for the following two most obvious reasons:

- If there is problem with the master VM template cloning procedure causing a BSOD on PVS target devices with error code 0x0000007B

- If you have an IP conflict arising in your DHCP scope causing a BSOD with error code 0x000000BC

The first reason is well documented in the Citrix Knowledge Center. This issue is more often reported on vSphere where the master VM doesn't seem to have any issue and boots fine. However, when the target devices boot from the standard vDisk, they receive the BSOD 0x0000007B error, as shown here:

```
A problem has been detected and Windows has been shut down to prevent damage
to your computer.

If this is the first time you've seen this stop error screen,
restart your computer. If this screen appears again, follow
these steps:

Check for viruses on your computer. Remove any newly installed
hard drives or hard drive controllers. Check your hard drive
to make sure it is properly configured and terminated.
Run CHKDSK /F to check for hard drive corruption, and then
restart your computer.

Technical information:

*** STOP: 0x0000007B (0xFFFFF880009A9928,0xFFFFFFFFC0000034,0x0000000000000000,0
x0000000000000000)
```

The issue is caused by an incorrect Ethernet PCI slot parameter and is a known issue with Citrix PVS 6.x.

The following steps help in resolving this issue:

1. Right-click on the target VM in the vCenter Console and select **Edit Properties**.

2. Click on **Options**. Then, select **General | Configuration Parameters**:

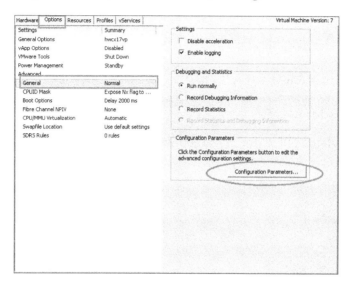

3. You should look for **ethernet0.pciSlotNumber** under the **Name** column and make a note of the value, shown in the following screenshot:

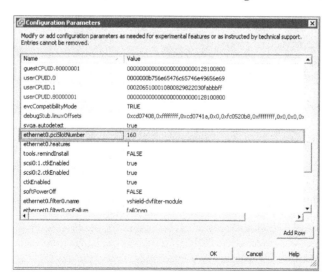

4. The value should match the value on the master VM. If the value doesn't exist on the master VM, create one as shown previously. Once created, use the PVS stream wizard to create more virtual machines using the updated master VM virtual machine.

 The solution is documented under Citrix article CTX133636; visit http://support.citrix.com/article/CTX133636 for more details.

The second reason is due to a duplicate IP being issued by your DHCP server to your target devices. The issue can also be due to incorrect DHCP configuration or a Ghost NIC on your Windows 7 VDIs.

Target devices when booted are presented with a BSOD error 0x000000BC, as shown here:

```
A problem has been detected and windows has been shut down to prevent damage
to your computer.

A duplicate IP address was assigned to this machine while attempting to
boot from the network.

If this is the first time you've seen this stop error screen,
restart your computer. If this screen appears again, follow
these steps:

Check to make sure any new hardware or software is properly installed.
If this is a new installation, ask your hardware or software manufacturer
for any windows updates you might need.

If problems continue, disable or remove any newly installed hardware
or software. Disable BIOS memory options such as caching or shadowing.
If you need to use Safe Mode to remove or disable components, restart
your computer, press F8 to select Advanced Startup Options, and then
select Safe Mode.

Technical information:

*** STOP: 0x000000BC (0x000000000D0BF70A,0x0000000010604BB4,0x000000004C9C0000,0
x0000000000000000)
```

The DHCP server issuing a duplicate IP to new machines often happens due to the deployment of two or more DHCP Relay Agent components for a Windows Server 2012-based DHCP Failover Cluster.

 This issue can also be resolved by installing the Windows RT, Windows 8, and Windows Server 2012 update rollup 2845533. For more details, visit https://support.microsoft.com/en-us/kb/2845533.

Target device failed to load BNIstack drivers

You might see this error on PVS target devices due to a Ghost NIC seen on Windows 7/Windows 2008 R2 machines built from VMWare templates when the template uses VMXNET3 as the network adapter.

You will see Event ID 7026, similar to this:

The following boot–start or system-start driver(s) failed to load:

bnistack

 To resolve this issue, remove the Ghost NIC from the master VM before installing PVS target device software. The resolution to the issue is documented under Citrix Knowledge Center article CTX133188. For more details, refer to the Citrix article at http://support.citrix.com/article/CTX133188.

Summary

We now have a good understanding of the Citrix MCS and PVS logging methods and how to analyze the service logs to troubleshoot any issue that comes our way.

In our next chapter, we will focus on XenDesktop integration with Citrix NetScaler.

11
Troubleshooting NetScaler® Integration Issues

In the last chapter, we discussed the troubleshooting of common MCS and PVS configuration issues that may arise in your Citrix XenDesktop environment in daily operations. We will now focus on troubleshooting some common issues that you may encounter while integrating Citrix NetScaler with your XenDesktop environment to enable remote access for users.

In this chapter, we will cover the following points:

- Integrating Citrix NetScaler with Citrix StoreFront
- NetScaler configuration
- Citrix StoreFront configuration to enable remote access
- Challenges with NetScaler integration

Integrating Citrix NetScaler® and Citrix StoreFront™

To configure Internet remote access for users who are geographically apart, you require Citrix NetScaler Gateway integrated with Citrix StoreFront to provide remote access to published applications and desktops.

Citrix has been doing this from a long time now. Initially, Citrix made use of its software based product called Citrix Secure Gateway, which was then changed to a more robust hardware appliance called Citrix Access Gateway.

However, all customers couldn't take advantage of Citrix Access Gateway due to its high cost as compared to the software version of Citrix Secure Gateway, which actually came free with the XenApp Enterprise license.

Due to customers' growing needs and demands, Citrix soon released a virtual appliance for Citrix Access Gateway commonly known as the CAG VPX appliance, which was later included as a feature in NetScaler ADC appliances. You can also opt for the NetScaler Gateway VPX appliance.

> With NetScaler Gateway and Citrix StoreFront, you can host multiple gateways on NetScaler pointing to different stores on the same StoreFront server. This was not possible with Citrix Web Interface servers.

Before we start with the integration, make sure that you meet the following prerequisites:

- Public and domain SSL certificates for NetScaler Gateway and Citrix StoreFront servers.
- Availability of NetScaler licenses
- A NetScaler appliance installed and ready with networking
- At least three IPs available to be used for integration

Let's get started with the NetScaler configuration.

Configuring NetScaler®

Once we are ready with the prerequisites and have either a NetScaler appliance installed in the data center or a VPX appliance imported on our Hypervisor, it is time to start configuring the NetScaler appliance according to the following steps:

1. Power on your NetScaler appliance and complete the initial configuration of setting IPv4 address, NetMask, and Gateway IPv4 address to create a default route, as shown in the following screenshot:

```
inetd cron httpd monit sshd .

!There is no ns.conf in the /nsconfig!

Start Netscaler software
tput: no terminal type specified and no TERM environmental variable.
Enter NetScaler's IPv4 address []: 192.168.1.3
Enter Netmask []: 255.255.255.0
Enter Gateway IPv4 address []: 192.168.1.1


Netscaler Virtual Appliance Initial Network Address Configuration.
This menu allows you to set and modify the initial IPv4 network addresses.
The current value is displayed in brackets ([]).
Selecting the listed number allows the address to be changed.

After the network changes are saved, you may either login as nsroot and
use the Netscaler command line interface, or use a web browser to
http://192.168.1.3 to complete or change the Netscaler configuration.

    1. NetScaler's IPv4 address [192.168.1.3]
    2. Netmask [255.255.255.0]
    3. Gateway IPv4 address [192.168.1.1]
    4. Save and quit
Select item (1-4) [4]: █
```

2. Once you are done, save and exit by opting for option 4 (type 4), as shown in the preceding screenshot.

3. The NetScaler device will then reboot. Once rebooted, browse to the NetScaler IPv4 address that we set in the previous step to open the GUI console. This is called NSIP (management IP for NetScaler).

With NetScaler 10.5, Citrix has removed the dependency on Java, which has been a big relief and a good news for all administrators. Due to enhanced Java security, the NetScaler GUI had faced a lot of issues and administrators were getting frustrated.

4. You are provided with default credentials, which are `nsroot` as username and `nsroot` again as password for the appliance. The login page is shown in the following screenshot:

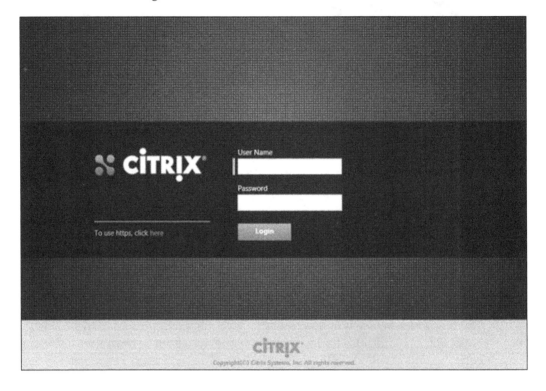

5. The console will directly take you to the configuration wizard to complete the remaining configuration in order to complete the NetScaler setup. The wizard will take you through setting up of the subnet IP, DNS IP addresses, and also through adding time zone, hostname, and licenses to the device, as shown in the following screenshot:

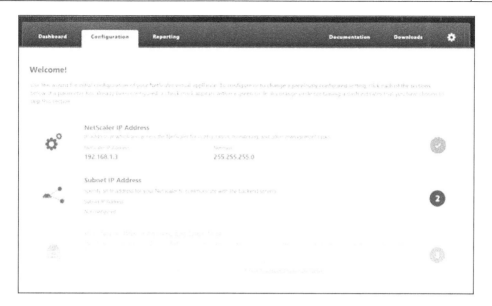

 Subnet IP address is used by NetScaler to communicate with the backend servers, using it as a source IP to proxy the client connections and send monitor probes to do a health check of backend servers.

6. Once done, reboot the device. This is required for licensing.

7. Once rebooted, check that your device has acquired the correct license and all features are licensed. For viewing license details, go to **System** and select **Licenses**:

Please make sure that if you are migrating your NetScaler appliances, you need to reallocate the NetScaler licenses (Platform and Enterprise licenses) as they are tied to the MAC address and hostname respectively. Otherwise, your devices will not pick up the licenses.

8. The next step is to create an SSL certificate. To create an SSL certificate, first you need to create an RSA key:

   1. Go to the **SSL** tab under **Traffic Management** and select **Create RSA Key**.

   2. Fill in the requested information, as shown.

   3. Make sure that you select key size equal to or higher than 1024 bits. The latest browsers don't trust SSL certificates that have 512-bit or lower encryption.

   4. Click on **OK**, once you are done.

9. Now we need to create a **Certificate Signing Request (CSR)**. To do this, click on **Create Certificate Signing Request (CSR)**:

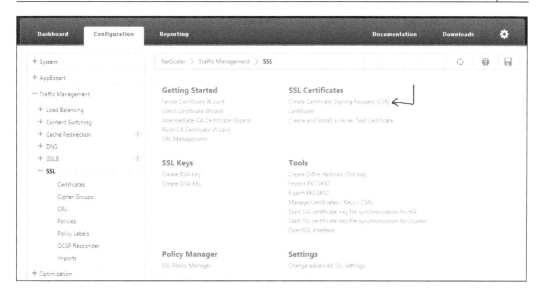

Fill in the required information as per your company or customer needs.
Once the information is populated, just click on **OK**:

10. To download the CSR file, click on **Manager Certificate** and then select **Download**:

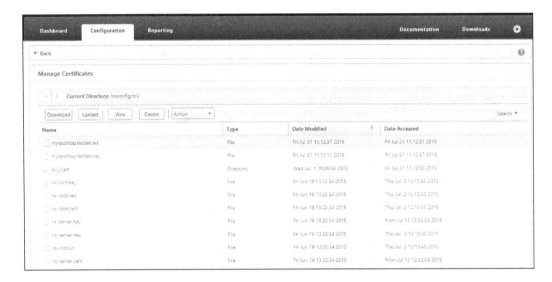

11. Now get your certificate generated by a third-party SSL certificate vendor, such as GoDaddy, VeriSign, or Thawte for the Apache server and get the certificate imported on your NetScaler appliance under the `/nsconfig/ssl` directory.

12. Once this is done, go to **Traffic Management | SSL | Certificates** and select **Install**. Fill in the information, as shown in the following screenshot and click on **OK**:

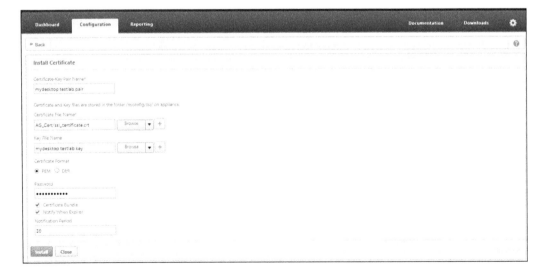

13. Now you will see a new certificate appearing along with the certificates of your NetScaler.

14. With the SSL part done, now we will configure the NetScaler Gateway for XenApp and XenDesktop. Click on **XenApp and XenDesktop** under the **Integrate with Citrix Products** tab, as shown in the following screenshot:

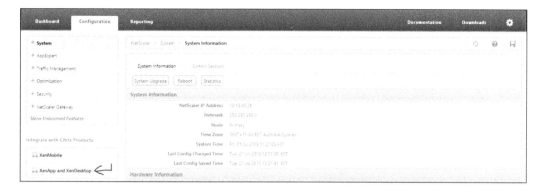

15. You will now be presented with a default checklist that you should review and make sure that you are ready with it. Once ready, click on **Get Started**:

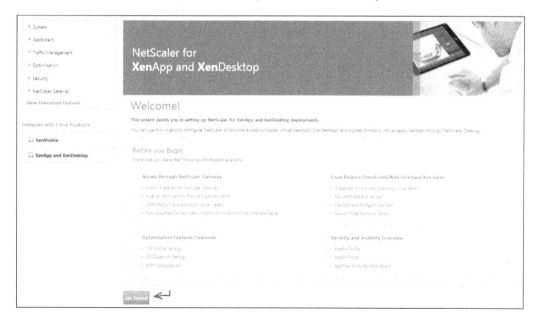

16. You will see a diagrammatic representation of your integration topology. We are doing a single-hop configuration here. Select **StoreFront** as your integration point from the drop-down menu and click on **Continue**, as shown in the following screenshot:

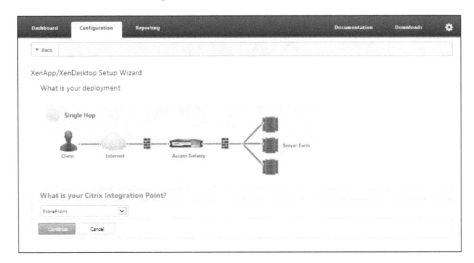

This wizard automatically discovers the deployment options to configure NetScaler Gateway. If your customer or your company has protected their internal networks using firewalls or created a DMZ, you will see an option to configure NS Gateway in double-hop deployment, as shown here:

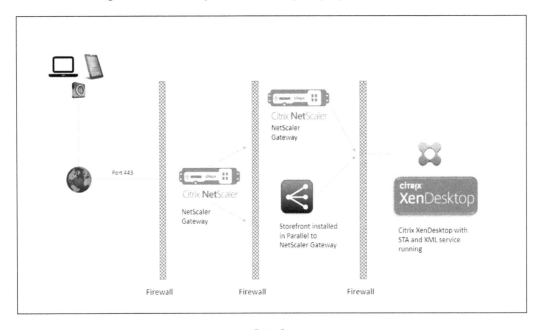

If the NetScaler Gateway is configured in a double-hop DMZ with StoreFront, then the e-mail-based autodiscovery for Receiver does not work. For more information about this deployment option, read the *Deploying NetScaler Gateway in a Double-Hop DMZ* article at `http://docs.citrix.com/en-us/netscaler-gateway/10-5/ng-advanced-wrapper-con/ng-double-dmz-wrapper-con.html`.

17. You will be asked to fill in the details to configure the NS Gateway virtual server. Fill in the required details and proceed:

18. Now you should bind the existing SSL certificate that we imported and installed on NetScaler appliance in the previous steps:

Click on **Continue** and Netscaler will check the certificate chain and if anything is missing, it will direct you to get the missing parts and complete the chain. This is a really cool new feature added.

19. After the SSL certificate is bound to the NetScaler Gateway virtual server, it is now time to configure the LDAP authentication server for Active Directory authentication:

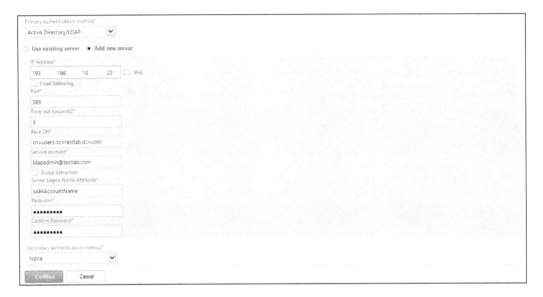

This will automatically create an LDAP policy and LDAP vServer. In the previous versions, we had to manually create an LDAP policy and LDAP vServer. We can still do it through the **Authentication** tab of the NetScaler Gateway.

 Similarly, you can configure Radius authentication vServer for secondary authentication. The Radius servers use a Radius key, which needs to be provided while configuring the Radius vServer.

20. Now we should be ready to configure our Citrix StoreFront server on NetScaler. You need to fill in the requested details and choose if you want to load balance StoreFront and XenDesktop controllers using the load balance vServer, as shown:

21. Now you can apply optimization policies, AppFW policies (if you have the license for it), and HDX Insight policies:

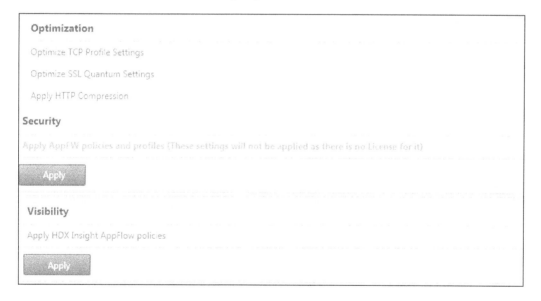

22. Once you apply the required policies, click on **Done**. It will ask for a reboot if you are applying TCP optimizations.

23. Now in NetScaler Gateway, go to **Global Settings** and select **Change Global Settings** and then go to the **Client Experience** tab and change the **UI Theme** option to **Green Bubble**:

24. We are done with the NetScaler Gateway configuration, you need to just save the configuration and reboot NetScaler.

The configuration shown in this section is based on the latest NetScaler 10.5 version; there could be a difference in the UI interface while configuring it on previous versions. So, refer to the Citrix Knowledge Center for the required version configuration.

Citrix StoreFront™ configuration for enabling remote access

We have configured our NetScaler appliance in the previous section to integrate with the XenDesktop environment. Now we need to enable the remote access on our Citrix StoreFront servers. The steps are as follows:

1. Log in to Citrix StoreFront server, open the StoreFront console, and navigate to the **Authentication** tab to select the appropriate authentication methods. We need to ensure that the **Pass through from NetScaler Gateway** option is checked:

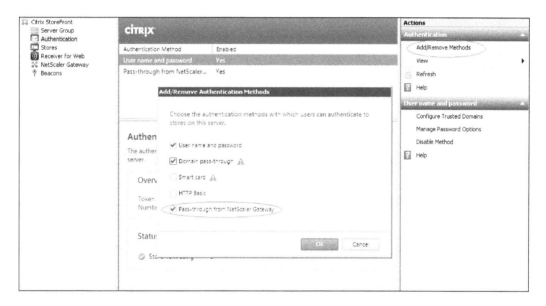

2. Now navigate to NetScaler Gateway and add the NetScaler appliance:

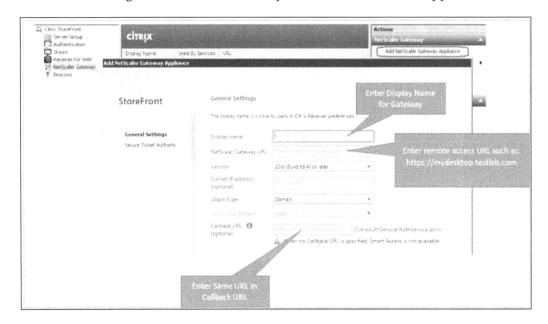

3. Click on **Secure Ticket Authority** and add STA servers:

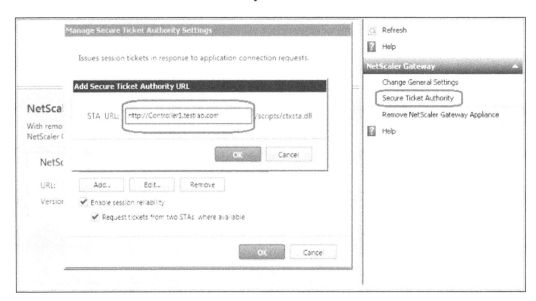

4. Now go to **Stores** and click on **Enable Remote Access**:

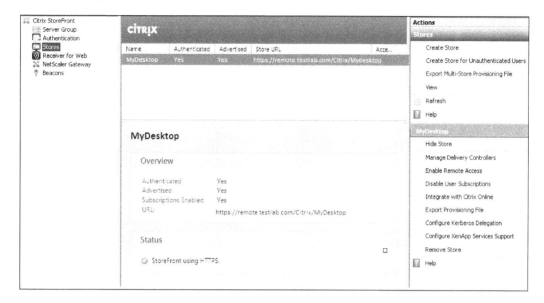

5. Select the **No VPN tunnel** option and select the previously created NetScaler Gateway:

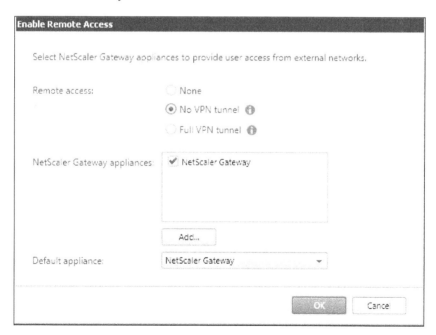

You are done and you can now browse the public URL using HTTPS:

> To bind your access gateway FQDN to the public IP, you need to create a public DNS entry. This can be done using the customer portal of your public SSL certificate vendor.

Challenges with NetScaler® integration

There are some common challenges that you might face while configuring Citrix NetScaler Gateway to enable remote access to your XenDesktop environment.

NATing and firewall configuration challenges

While configuring the NetScaler Gateway in one-arm mode, we will assign a private IP to the NetScaler Gateway vServer. For requests that come from Internet to this private IP, you need to configure the route and open an SSL port to allow communication.

We should not forget two important tasks here:

- We need to make sure that network admin performs NAT for the public IP to the vServer private IP over ports 443 and 80 (to allow HTTP to HTTPS redirection)
- The firewall should be configured to receive 443/80 TCP traffic on the NS Gateway vServer private IP

If you have configured your network and firewall configuration as suggested here, you should all be set up to reach the NS Gateway VPN logon page from Internet. Any misconfiguration in the preceding components can result in HTTP errors for your users.

SSL certificates and challenges

When it comes to SSL certificates, we need to make sure that we have the appropriate SSL certificates installed on the following components:

- Citrix NetScaler
- Citrix StoreFront

NetScaler 10.5 has made identifying the issues related to the SSL certificate chain very easy, as described earlier in the NetScaler configuration steps. However, you might struggle if you are using a NetScaler version lower than 10.5 and have not installed the public SSL certificate keypair properly:

While installing the SSL certificate keypair on NetScaler, always remember to create a certificate bundle that includes the complete certificate chain. Also, make sure that while downloading the SSL certificate from the CA website, you select the Apache Server and not IIS:

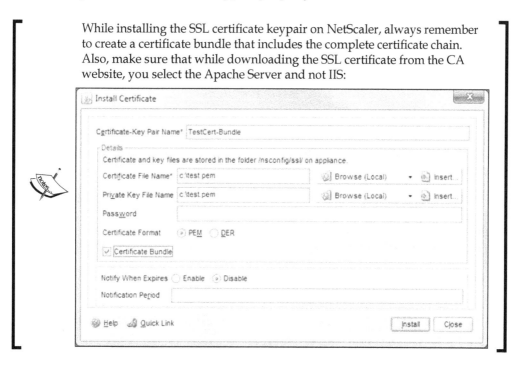

There are some common errors that you may encounter if your SSL certificates are misconfigured on the Citrix NetScaler or Citrix StoreFront components. The errors are as follows:

The server certificate received is not trusted – SSL Error 61

SSL Error 61 suggests that the NetScaler device doesn't have the required CA root certificate to establish trust with the SSL certificate, as shown in the following screenshot. However, you may find that you already have a CA root certificate installed on the device and this error is noticed only when using a Citrix Receiver. If you downgrade the receiver to Online Plug-in, this issue goes away.

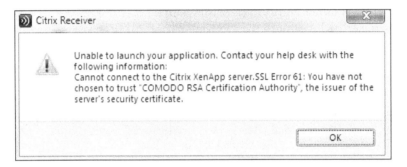

This happens when your third-party CA issues an SSL certificate that is not compliant with RFC 3280 instructions for the Enhanced Key Usage field. The NetScaler Gateway acts as an SSL server, so server authentication (`1.3.6.1.5.5.7.3.1`) must be listed among the designated key uses if any are present.

If the Extended Key Usage field is not present in the certificate, the certificate might be considered valid. Many SSL certificate vendors already have their SSL cert root installed on operating system vendors but sometimes the issue arises due to incorrect SSL certificate issued to the customer.

You can request your CA vendor to reissue the certificate and get it corrected.

An underlying problem when establishing the SSL/TLS trust relationship

You may encounter this problem when you are using a self-signed certificate on Citrix StoreFront servers. Citrix StoreFront doesn't like self-signed certificates and may break the trust relationship.

It is recommended to install domain certificates issued by an internal CA authority to avoid any such issues.

NetScaler® callback URL configuration

One of the important components of NetScaler integration is to set the **Callback URL** option properly:

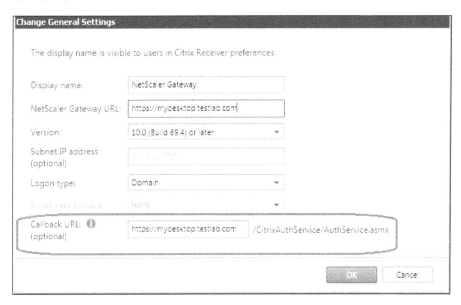

You may encounter a *Cannot complete your request* error during the StoreFront logon if the callback URL is not set properly. It is recommended to always set the callback URL same as the FQDN to which the certificate is issued.

 Don't forget to add a host entry on the StoreFront servers to point the FQDN of your NetScaler Gateway URL to the private IP address of your NS Gateway vServer or create a DNS entry to resolve the FQDN to the NetScaler Gateway vServer private IP.

Securing XenApp®/XenDesktop® communication

You might want to secure the communication between your XenDesktop Delivery Controller and StoreFront communication and you can use HTTPS for the same:

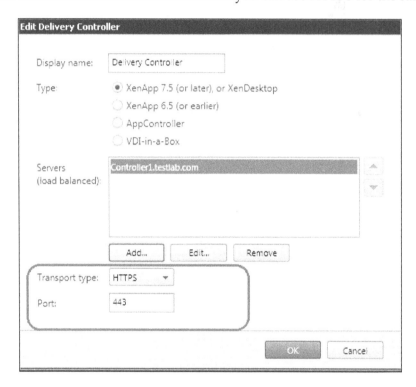

You need to install the SSL certificate on Delivery Controllers and then change the configuration on the StoreFront server to use HTTPS to communicate to Delivery Controllers. However, you might encounter an issue where no users will be able to see any of their published applications or desktops based on the delivery groups.

This is a known issue with Windows Server 2012 R2 having security update KB2919355. This update actually changed the cipher suite due to which the Delivery Controller stops all HTTPS communication.

To work around this issue, you need to get a GPO created and implemented on the Delivery Controllers' OU. The steps for this are as follows:

1. Create a new GPO.
2. Browse to **Computer Configuration** | **Administrative Templates** | **Network** | **SSL Configuration Settings** | **SSL Cipher Suite Order**.
3. Enable this policy.

Once enabled, users will be able to see their apps.

Summary

We should now have a good understanding of the NetScaler configuration and its integration with Citrix StoreFront to enable remote access for your VDI deployments. Also, we have covered the basic challenges that should help you troubleshoot and fix integration issues for Citrix components.

In our next chapter, we will focus on dealing with the known issues concerning Citrix XenDesktop and how to work around these issues to get a successful VDI deployment.

12

Dealing with Known Issues in Citrix XenDesktop®

In the last chapter, we discussed the integration of Citrix NetScaler with our XenDesktop environment to enable remote access for users and also the common challenges that you may encounter while doing the integration.

We have covered almost all the troubleshooting topics in our last 11 chapters in Citrix XenDesktop environment. We will now be looking at some general issues that have been identified and recorded by Citrix in their database. These are the issues that every admin must be aware of before starting troubleshooting other Citrix XenDesktop issues.

Known Citrix XenDesktop® general issues

There are many issues that have been discovered with Citrix XenDesktop 7.6. We will cover the basic and general issues that every administrator should be aware of and they are listed in the following section.

We are referring to the latest version, many issues that were reported with the previous versions have been resolved with this release. You can always refer to the Citrix Knowledge Center for a particular version's known issues by visiting http://docs.citrix.com.

The CreateAnonymousUserApp tool doesn't delete anonymous user accounts

The tool deletes only the user profiles and passwords and not the users, as these users are local to the server they are not deleted with the tool. As a workaround, you need to delete the users from the computer management console manually.

You cannot change the SOAP/HTTP port for Citrix Universal Print Server web service

Citrix recommends that you change the port using PowerShell cmdlets. To set a session printer policy, use the following command:

```
Set-ItemProperty LocalGpo:\Computer\Unfiltered\Settings\ICA\Printing\
UniversalPrintServer\UpsHttpPort -name Value -Value <portnumber>
```

Known Hyper-V host limitations

If a Hyper-V host is paused and then resumed from a paused state, the state does not get updated immediately by System Center Virtual Machine Manager servers and it might fail catalog creation or cause other issues for Machine Creation Services.

 It is always recommended to refresh the Hyper-V host node before performing any MCS admin tasks or you can also run environment tests to avoid any communication issues.

The Enhanced Desktop Experience policy setting does not affect pre-existing user or administrator profiles

You need to delete all the pre-existing profiles before enabling this setting in the Citrix policies. You need to also delete the profile used for VDA installation once it has been completed on the server or desktop.

No support for the RemoteFX vGPU feature on a Hyper-V host

Citrix XenDesktop 7.6 doesn't support the use of the RemoteFX vGPU feature on Hyper-V hosts. We need to use RDP to access the RemoteFX functionality such as Hyper-V vGPU.

RDP connections to the VDIs are not recommended

If multiple users make an RDP and ICA connection to one of the windows desktop and if the RDP user locks the desktop screen, the user with ICA session cannot log in to the desktop. In this case, you need to log off the user RDP session forcefully in order to allow ICA sessions.

Session sharing can't be disabled

You can't disable session sharing in XenApp 7.6 even through registry. This is enabled by default and if you try to disable it with the registry key, the first application will launch whereas the subsequent applications will fail to launch. There is no workaround for this issue.

Windows Server 2012 memory leak issue

If the user connects and disconnects to their session frequently to work from home and mobile locations, it will cause memory leaks with the `DWM.exe` process in Windows Server 2012 and can even cause the server to get exhausted and crash. This is a known issue in Microsoft code.

 For more details on this issue, visit `https://support.microsoft.com/en-us/kb/2855336`.

Profile management delay

Enabling the profile management feature and running logon scripts in an environment can cause Windows Server 2012 R2 or Windows 8.1 to delay login by up to five minutes. Once the session is established, you won't be able to see the logon duration for logon scripts in the Director console. However, you can control the delay by using the **Configure Logon Script Delay** policy that is set to 0 by default.

Windows 8.1 desktop launch issue

There is a known issue with Windows 8.1 desktop launch when Microsoft software update management enabled. To work around this issue, follow these steps:

1. Go to the Windows 8.1 **Taskbar and Navigation properties** dialog box.

2. In the **Navigation** tab, select all the options in the **Start screen** section, as shown in the following screenshot:

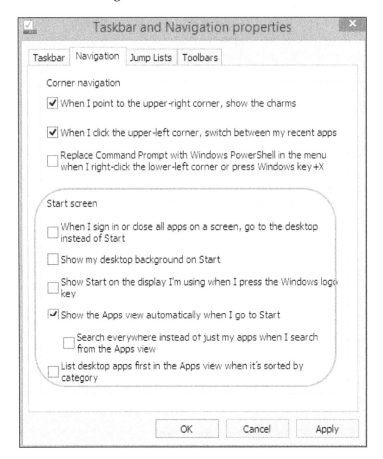

License error while opening an RDP session to a brokered session

You may see an error, such as: *You cannot access the session because there are no licenses available*, while connecting to a brokered session using RDP. To work around this issue, disable the settings described here.

Open the `Default.ICA` file on Citrix StoreFront server by browsing to the `C:\inetpub\wwwroot\Citrix\Store\App_data` location and then disable the following settings:

- `RDPConnection=False`
- `RDP-RedirectDrives=False`
- `RDP-RedirectDynamicDrives=False`

The Persistent Cache Policy setting is incorrectly configured as Kbps

The value is actually in **bits per second** (**bps**) and not Kbps.

Connecting timeout failure

The maximum connection timer and disconnect timer settings might not work correctly on Windows Server 2012 machines containing Windows Server OS VDAs; hence, causing unexpected session timeout behavior.

Citrix Generic Universal Printer autocreation issue

When the **Auto-create Generic Universal Printer** policy is enabled, `CpSvc.exe` might not create the printer automatically. You need to apply the hotfix to address this issue. For hotfix details, refer Citrix Knowledge Center articles CTX141565 and CTX141566.

Maximum allowed color depth failure on Windows 2012 R2 Server OS VDAs

Do not enable the **Maximum Allowed Color Depth** policy if you have Windows 2012 R2 Server OS VDAs in your environment. It may affect the user connections to the XenApp server, as color depth doesn't apply on the machines using WDDM as a display driver.

Citrix Studio console issue

You might see MMC crashing if you attempt to launch Citrix Studio and Citrix StoreFront console. This happens if you have XenApp and XenDesktop software installed on a single Windows 2008 SP1 server. To work around this issue, you need to update native image generator. The command to do this is as follows:

```
ngen update /force
```

This may take several minutes to complete.

Long names with machine catalogs and storage paths cause disk errors

There is a maximum limit of 255 characters for the length of the file path for the VM resources identified by Microsoft. This issue has been reported while using local storage on a standalone Hyper-V host, due to the long file path used to store the VMs. However, it is not limited to standalone Hyper-V hosts.

To work around this issue, always create VMM MCS catalogs with relatively short names, especially when the storage is accessed using a long path. If possible, try to shorten the storage path where the VMs are stored.

Citrix ICA® listener connection timeout policy issue

Citrix ICA listener connection timeouts apply to VDAs 5.0, 5.5, and 5.6 FP1. These don't apply to VDA 7.0, 7.1, 7.5, and 7.6 even if Studio policies say so. This is a known issue.

User devices unable to connect to Windows 2012 R2 OS VDA using a HTML5 receiver

To avoid this issue, don't use the Master Image (either MCS or PVS) to create new a Server OS VDA machine. Alternatively, you can modify the following registry entries to work around this issue:

- `HKEY_LOCAL_MACHINE\Software\Citrix\GroupPolicy\Defaults\ IcaPolicies\AcceptWebSocketsConnections = 1`

- `HKEY_LOCAL_MACHINE\Software\Citrix\GroupPolicy\Defaults\ IcaPolicies\AllowDesktopLaunchForNonAdmins = 1`

- `HKEY_LOCAL_MACHINE\Software\Citrix\GroupPolicy\Defaults\ IcaPolicies\WebSocketsPort = 8008`

If you have a machine with issues that was created using Citrix Provisioning Services, follow the recommendations in the article CTX139265.

 For complete list of known issues with the Citrix XenDesktop product suite, visit `http://docs.citrix.com/en-us/ xenapp-and-xendesktop/7-6/xad-whats-new/xad- xaxd76-knownissues.html`.

Summary

With this chapter, we have now come to an end of this wonderful troubleshooting book. You should now have a good understanding of the basic issues related to the XenDesktop product and how to work around these issues.

It has been a great pleasure to write this troubleshooting book to help you gain the required skills on troubleshooting the Citrix XenDesktop environment. I hope that the skills acquired in this book will help you to resolve Citrix XenDesktop issues with confidence. Thank you for reading this book and happy troubleshooting.

Index

Thank you for buying
Troubleshooting Citrix XenDesktop®

About Packt Publishing

Packt, pronounced 'packed', published its first book, *Mastering phpMyAdmin for Effective MySQL Management*, in April 2004, and subsequently continued to specialize in publishing highly focused books on specific technologies and solutions.

Our books and publications share the experiences of your fellow IT professionals in adapting and customizing today's systems, applications, and frameworks. Our solution-based books give you the knowledge and power to customize the software and technologies you're using to get the job done. Packt books are more specific and less general than the IT books you have seen in the past. Our unique business model allows us to bring you more focused information, giving you more of what you need to know, and less of what you don't.

Packt is a modern yet unique publishing company that focuses on producing quality, cutting-edge books for communities of developers, administrators, and newbies alike. For more information, please visit our website at www.packtpub.com.

About Packt Enterprise

In 2010, Packt launched two new brands, Packt Enterprise and Packt Open Source, in order to continue its focus on specialization. This book is part of the Packt Enterprise brand, home to books published on enterprise software – software created by major vendors, including (but not limited to) IBM, Microsoft, and Oracle, often for use in other corporations. Its titles will offer information relevant to a range of users of this software, including administrators, developers, architects, and end users.

Writing for Packt

We welcome all inquiries from people who are interested in authoring. Book proposals should be sent to author@packtpub.com. If your book idea is still at an early stage and you would like to discuss it first before writing a formal book proposal, then please contact us; one of our commissioning editors will get in touch with you.

We're not just looking for published authors; if you have strong technical skills but no writing experience, our experienced editors can help you develop a writing career, or simply get some additional reward for your expertise.

Citrix XenDesktop® Cookbook
Third Edition

ISBN: 978-1-78217-517-9   Paperback: 430 pages

Over 40 engaging recipes that will help you implement a full-featured XenDesktop® 7.6 architecture and its main satellite components

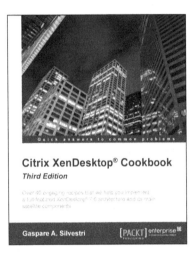

1. Implement, configure, and optimize the migration from a physical to a VDI architecture using XenDesktop 7.6.

2. Publish desktops and applications to the end user devices, optimizing their performance and increasing the security for the delivered resources.

Mastering Citrix® XenDesktop®

ISBN: 978-1-78439-397-7   Paperback: 484 pages

Design and implement a high performance and efficient virtual desktop infrastructure using Citrix® XenDesktop®

1. Design, deploy, configure, optimize, troubleshoot, and maintain XenDesktop for enterprise environments and to meet emerging high-end business requirements.

2. Configure Citrix XenDesktop to deliver a rich virtual desktop experience to end users.

3. A comprehensive, practical guide to monitoring a XenDesktop environment and automating XenDesktop tasks using PowerShell.

Please check **www.PacktPub.com** for information on our titles

Citrix® XenApp® 7.x
Performance Essentials

Luca Dentella

Citrix® XenApp® 7.x Performance Essentials

ISBN: 978-1-78217-611-4   Paperback: 120 pages

Tune and optimize the performance of your farms with the new improved XenApp® architecture

1. Monitor your infrastructure using the new tools, and learn how to optimize the end-user experience.

2. Discover the new FlexCast Management Architecture of XenApp 7.5 and its components.

3. Explore the new features designed for mobile and remote users.

Citrix® XenApp® 6.5
Expert Cookbook

Esther Barthel MSc

Citrix® XenApp® 6.5 Expert Cookbook

ISBN: 978-1-84968-522-1   Paperback: 420 pages

Over 125 recipes that enable you to configure, administer, and troubleshoot a XenApp® infrastructure for effective application virtualization

1. Create installation scripts for Citrix XenApp, License Servers, Web Interface, and StoreFront.

2. Use PowerShell scripts to configure and administer the XenApp's infrastructure components.

3. Discover Citrix and community written tools to maintain a Citrix XenApp infrastructure.

Please check **www.PacktPub.com** for information on our titles

www.ingramcontent.com/pod-product-compliance
Lightning Source LLC
Chambersburg PA
CBHW060530060326
40690CB00017B/3447

* 9 7 8 1 7 8 5 2 8 0 1 3 9 *